Taharas Halashon

A GUIDE TO THE LAWS
OF *LASHON HARA*
AND *RECHILUS*

Taharas Halashon

A GUIDE TO THE LAWS
OF *LASHON HARA*
AND *RECHILUS*

arranged by
Ze'ev Greenwald

translated by
David Landesman

FELDHEIM PUBLISHERS *Jerusalem / New York*

For questions regarding this book write to:
Ze'ev Greenwald
POB 43015
Jerusalem
02-527-417

First published 1994
Copyright © 1994 by Ze'ev Greenwald

All rights reserved.
No part of this publication may be
translated, reproduced, stored in a retrieval
system or transmitted, in any form or by any
means, electronic, mechanical, photocopying,
recording or otherwise, without prior permission
in writing from the publishers.

FELDHEIM PUBLISHERS
POB 35002/Jerusalem, Israel

200 Airport Executive Park
Spring Valley, NY 10977

Printed in Israel

Table of Contents

THE LAWS OF *LASHON HARA*

1. What Constitutes *Lashon Hara*? — 11
2. The Severity of Speaking *Lashon Hara*? — 25
3. About Whom and to Whom May one Not Speak *Lashon Hara*? — 33
4. *Lashon Hara* That is True or That Causes No Damage — 45
5. *Lashon Hara* That is Not Related Through Speech — 55
6. *Avak Lashon Hara* — 63
7. Accepting *Lashon Hara* — 73
8. Listening to *Lashon Hara* — 85
9. *Lashon Hara* Spoken for a Purpose — 93
10. *Lashon Hara* Spoken in Front of Three People or in a Subject's Presence — 103
11. Avoiding and Repenting for the Sin of *Lashon Hara* — 115

THE LAWS OF *RECHILUS*

12. What is the Prohibition of *Rechilus* (Gossip)? — 127
13. When Does the Prohibition of *Rechilus* Apply? — 139
14. Avoiding *Rechilus* — 147
15. The Prohibition of Accepting *Rechilus* — 155
16. The Laws Regarding *Rechilus* Spoken for a Purpose — 167

Recommendations

הרב חיים פנחס שיינברג
ראש ישיבת "תורה אור"
ומורה הוראה דקרית מטרסדורף
ירושלים

בס"ד מנחם אב תשנ"א

באתי בדברי אלו לסייע לפועלו של הרב זאב גרינולד שליט"א שחיבר ספר על הלכות לשון הרע ורכילות בשם "טהרת הלשון".

חומרתו של עוון לשה"ר והזכות הגדולה של שמירת הלשון הביאו לחיבור ספרים רבים וחשובים בענין זה. מעלת הספר "טהרת הלשון" היא הבהירות הרבה של ההלכות. הסדר שבו מסייע ללימוד, שינון וזכירה בצורה קלה. תועלת רבה תצמח בס"ד למעיין בספר.
אברך את המחבר שספרו יזכה להשיג את מטרתו בקודש ושיזכה לחבר עוד ספרים לתועלת הרבים.

חיים פנחס שיינברג

Recommendations

ישיבת "כנסת חזקיהו"
ת.ד. 7 כפר חסידים

בס"ד ט"ו מנחם אב תשנ"א

לכב' ידידי הדגול, נעים המידות, יראת השם היא אוצרו הרה"ג רבי זאב גרינולד שליט"א.

אחרי שכבר זכה לחבר כמה ספרים חשובים, נדבו לבו הטהור לחבר ספר בעניין העומד ברומו של עולם, הלא הוא שמירת הלשון אשר "מות וחיים ביד הלשון". וכמה עמל יטרח ומסר נפשו רבן של ישראל בעל החפץ חיים זצ"ל למען חזק עניין זה בישראל. ואע"פ שכבר נתחברו כמה ספרים בעניין זה בדור האחרון - מצא שעדיין יש מקום לספר שיכתב בצורה קלה ובצורה נעימה ומובן גודל התועלת בזה.

ויהי רצון שספרו ירבה את ידיעת ההלכות ושמירת הלשון ויקרב את גאולתנו ויזכה לחבר עוד ספרים חשובים. ומעלין בקודש.

אוהבו ומכבדו,
דב יפה

Nachman Bulman   נחמן בולמן

ב"ה ב' טבת תשנ"ג

Periodically, Torah works appear, from the pen of R. Zéev Greenwald, which enrich and inspire thousands of readers and students. R. Greenwald brings to bear broad scholarship on works of popular appeal. He writes with clarity, brevity and guidance for practical application.

His "Gates of Halacha" has won a broad readership. Now, there is to be published his work on "Taharas Halashon" (Purity of Speech) together with his "Gates of Halacha", in a fine English rendition — which was done by a much praised translator and author in his own right — R. David Landesman.

R. Greenwald's works are much needed in our times, and many are his grateful readers and students.

נאם נחמן בולמן — נחמן בולמן, סלה טבת תשנ"ג

Preface

Many books have been printed in recent times on the laws of *Lashon Hara* and *Rechilus*. Every publication added its own noteworthy contribution towards the observance of refined speech and the avoidance of deprecatory talk. The goal of this present volume is to facilitate understanding, incorporating, and memorizing these laws by an easy division according to topics.

Many quotes from our sages and our holy books were included in the book. These quotes speak about the seriousness of the prohibition of derogatory speech, the value of watching one's speech, and the great reward that accrues to one who is heedful of these prohibitions.

In the last chapter, questions and answers are provided to help the reader summarize and review the contents of the book. We hope that this chapter will help the reader to gain command of the laws of watching one's speech.

◆◆◆

To all the individuals who participated in the publication of this book and helped see it through to its completion, our heartfelt thanks and appreciation.

We pray to Hashem that no halachic misunderstanding should arise through this book. May this book succeed in encouraging many to be heedful of forbidden talk.

CHAPTER 1

What constitutes *Lashon Hara*?

Forms of speech prohibited as *Lashon Hara*

> Many people, on the Day of Accounting, will be shown a list of their meritorious deeds. Failing to recognize some of them, they will say, "We never did this!" They will be told that the deeds were done by people who spoke derogatorily about them. Similarly, when those who spoke derogatorily find that deeds which they had performed are not accounted for, they will wonder what has become of them. They will be told, "They were removed from your account and credited to that of the person about whom you spoke derogatorily." In addition, they will find records of evil actions that they never did. When they say, "We never did this," they will be informed that those actions were debited to them because they had spoken badly about someone.
>
> *Chovos Halevavos, Sha'ar Hakniah 7*

WHAT IS *LASHON HARA* ?

1. Speaking derogatorily about another person.[1]

   The Torah prohibits speaking derogatorily about someone:

   ◆ even though no harm is caused as a result.[2]

   ◆ even if the speaker is certain that no harm will result in the future.

2. Speech which may cause damage to another person or to his property or that may cause him pain or frighten him.[3]

   ◆ Speech which can cause any form of monetary damage, pain or embarrassment is prohibited even if it is not derogatory.

---

1. *Chafetz Chaim*, Vol. I, 1:1; 5:1-2
2. *Chafetz Chaim*, Vol. I, 3:6
3. *Chafetz Chaim* Vol. I, 3:6

SUBJECTS INCLUDED IN THE PROHIBITION OF *LASHON HARA*

Derogatory speech about a person encompasses many areas. On the following pages, we shall outline a number of them, including:

♦ references to the actions of a person's ancestors or to that person's actions in the past.

♦ references to *mitzvos* and prohibitions between man and G-d.

♦ references to *mitzvos* and prohibitions between man and his fellow man.

♦ references to a person's character traits.

> Hashem said to Israel: "My beloved sons, am I lacking something that I must ask you to provide it? And what do I request of you? That you love each other, that you respect one another and that you show fear for one another."
>
> *Tanna D'vei Eliyahu*, end of Chapter 28

SUBJECTS INCLUDED IN THE PROHIBITION OF *LASHON HARA*

1. References to the actions of a person's ancestors or relatives.[1]

For example:
- "Reuven's father was known as a corrupt person."
- "I knew Shimon's grandfather. It was difficult to do business with him."

2.. References to a person's previous actions.[1]

For example:
- "As a child, he was not considered a serious student."
- "Until a few years ago, he was not as careful about observing *mitzvos* as he is now."

These types of references are derogatory[1] and serve no purpose.[2]

The person being spoken about may have changed and one may not speak about his past mistakes nor about those of his ancestors.

---

1. *Chafetz Chaim*, Vol. I, 4:1
2. See Chapter 10 regarding *lashon hara* spoken for a purpose.

SUBJECTS INCLUDED IN THE PROHIBITION OF *LASHON HARA*

3. References to *mitzvos* or prohibitions between man and G-d.[1] For example:

- One may not relate that a person violated or failed to fulfill a Torah prohibition or requirement (e.g., that he does not learn Torah or that he is in the habit of lying. It should be noted that though this type of speech is quite common and the potential embarrassment is consequently less, it is still *lashon hara*.)[2]

- One may not relate that a person is not observant in fulfilling the details of *mitzvos* (e.g., that he is miserly or that he does not properly honor the Sabbath).[2]

- One may not relate that a person is negligent in fulfilling Rabbinical enactments according to the preferred way of doing them.[2]

Even if these things are true, it is still prohibited as *lashon hara*. One should assume that the person either inadvertently failed to act properly, did not know that his actions were prohibited or assumed that the prohibition which he violated was only an optional stringency.[3]

---
1. *Chafetz Chaim*, Vol. I, 4:1
2. *Chafetz Chaim*, Vol. I, 4:2
3. *Chafetz Chaim*, Vol. I, 4:3

SUBJECTS INCLUDED IN THE PROHIBITION OF LASHON HARA

4. References to *mitzvos* or prohibitions between man and his fellow man.[1]

For example:

- One may not relate that a person refuses to grant loans.

- One may not relate that a person is unkind or refuses to extend help to others.

- One may not relate that a person is vengeful.

- One may not relate that a person is contentious in business or takes unfair advantage of others.[2]

---

1. *Chafetz Chaim*, Vol. I, 5:1. See Chapter 10 regarding speaking *lashon hara* for a purpose.
2. *Chafetz Chaim*, Vol. I, 4; *Be'er Mayim Chayim* 3

SUBJECTS INCLUDED IN THE PROHIBITION OF *LASHON HARA*

5. Disparaging a person for lacking a quality which everyone desires to possess.

Regarding Torah learning:[1]

♦ One may not say about a person who is considered to be a Torah scholar, that he is lacking expertise in a certain subject area.

By doing so, one may lessen the respect that he commands as well as cause him monetary damage. Furthermore, this type of speech causes the honor of the Torah itself to be diminished.

♦ One may not say that a rabbi or a Torah educator is not a Torah scholar.

Aside from the personal affront to the person about whom one is speaking, this type of speech causes the honor of Torah to be diminished and may well result in a general decline in the level of religious observance.

---

1. *Chafetz Chaim*, Vol. I, 5:4

SUBJECTS INCLUDED IN THE PROHIBITION OF *LASHON HARA*

6. Disparaging a person for lacking a quality which everyone desires to possess.

As regards wisdom:[1]

♦ One may not say that a person is unintelligent.

Doing so can cause anguish or even real loss. For example, if the person about whom one spoke is not married, a potential mate may decide to avoid marrying him because of what was said. Similarly, if the person is in business, people may decide not to deal with him.

As regards physical strength:[2]

♦ One may not say that a person is weak.

Doing so can cause the person substantial loss. For example, if he is a salaried worker and his employer hears that he is physically weak, he might lose his job.

---

1. *Chafetz Chaim*, Vol. I, 5:2
2. *Chafetz Chaim*, Vol. I, 5:5

SUBJECTS INCLUDED IN THE PROHIBITION OF *LASHON HARA*

7. Disparaging a person for lacking a quality which everyone desires to possess.

As regards skills:[1]

♦ One may not say that a person is not skilled in his work.

Doing so may cause real loss, for as a result people may be reluctant to hire him.

As regards goods:[2]

♦ One may not speak derogatorily about the goods that a person sells.

For example, one may not say that the goods sold by a specific storekeeper are inferior because, by doing so, one may cause him substantial loss.
(This type of speech is quite common among competitors.)

---

1. *Chafetz Chaim*, Vol. I, 5:4
2. *Chafetz Chaim*, Vol. I, 5:7

SUBJECTS INCLUDED IN THE PROHIBITION OF *LASHON HARA*

8. Disparaging a person for lacking a quality which everyone desires to possess.

As regards wealth:[1]

♦ One may not say that a person is not as wealthy as people think or that he is in a great deal of debt.

Doing so may cause people to cease lending him money or extending credit.

As regards a person's character:[2]

♦ One may not say that a person is haughty or angers quickly.

It is possible that the person sincerely regrets that he has bad habits or he may be unaware of the prohibitions that pertain to such negative character traits.

---

1. *Chafetz Chaim*, Vol. I, 5:5
2. *Chafetz Chaim*, Vol. I, 4:9

WHEN THE IMPLICATION OF THE STATEMENT DEPENDS UPON WHOM ONE IS SPEAKING

The same conversation can be complimentary when told about Reuven and derogatory when told about Shimon.[1]

COMPLIMENT	THE STORY	DEROGATORY
If the subject has to work long hours to earn a living.	He learns Torah three hours a day.	If the subject has a considerable amount of free time.
If the subject is poor.	He gave x amount of money to *tzedakah* or to purchase food for *Shabbos*.	If the subject is wealthy.
If the subject is a simple person.	Describing how he treats his employees.	If the subject is a person of great moral reputation.

Similar statements which constitute a compliment for Reuven and disparagement for Shimon encompass all areas of life.

---

1. *Chafetz Chaim*, Vol. I, 4:6

"GENTEEL" LASHON HARA

The prohibition of *lashon hara* includes speaking about a person as if one did not know that the subject discussed was *lashon hara*, or relating something without mentioning names when it is common knowledge that the story concerns a specific individual.[1]

> *Do not say to the angel that it was inadvertent*
> (*Koheles* 5:5)
>
> [This means that] one should not say [to himself], "I will speak *lashon hara* and no one will know." Hashem says to this person, "Know that I have sent an angel, and he stands beside you and records everything that you say about others." From where is this derived? The verse (*Koheles* 10:20) states: *Even in your thoughts do not curse a king*. Why? *Because the birds in the sky shall carry the voice* (ibid.) And what is meant by *the ones with wings will retell* (ibid.)? This refers to the angels, of whom it states (*Yeshaya* 6:2); *And they had six wings, six wings behind them.*
>
> *Devarim Rabbah* 6:5

---
1. *Chafetz Chaim* Vol. 1, 3:5

CHAPTER 2

The severity of speaking *Lashon Hara*

Examples where the severity of the prohibition of *Lashon Hara* is particularly great

> "And the most important manner in which one can earn a place in the world to come is to guard one's speech. And this is greater than all the Torah and good deeds, for speech is the holiest of the holy.
>
> *Iggeres HaGra*

THE *BAAL LASHON HARA*

A person who regularly speaks *lashon hara* and makes no attempt to try to refrain from committing this sin, is referred to by our Sages as a

baal lashon hara

(literally a master of *lashon hara*) and his punishment is most severe.

> Our Sages said: There are three sins for which man is punished in this world and which [also] preclude his receiving a portion in the world to come. They are: worshipping false gods, incestuous relationships and murder, and [the prohibition of speaking] *lashon hara* is equivalent to all of them. And the Sages brought proof from Scripture [to support this opinion]. And our early masters explained that they were referring to those who had become accustomed to constantly violating this prohibition and who make no attempt to refrain, for they view it as being permissible.
>
> *Chafetz Chaim*, Vol. 1, 1:4

SPEAKING *LASHON HARA* IN PUBLIC

The more people who hear one speaking *lashon hara*, the greater the sin of the speaker, for he causes more people to transgress.[1]

Therefore, one who regularly speaks in public — e.g., a lecturer or teacher — should be exceedingly careful to refrain from saying anything that is derogatory when speaking.

> Man's power of speech is a spiritual force and it has great effect in the higher spheres. Consequently, the damage wrought by improper speech in the higher worlds is severe and awesome. And the greater the damage, the greater is the punishment.
>
> *Shmiras Halashon, Sha'ar Hazchirah*, Chapter I

---

1. *Chafetz Chaim*, Introduction, 4th Prohibition

TWO PEOPLE WHO SPEAK *LASHON HARA*

The sin is even greater if two people speak *lashon hara*. The person listening will give greater credence if two people tell the same story than he would have had only one person told the story. Consequently, the damage caused is greater.[1]

> Rabbi Elazar ben Parta taught: Come and see the [negative] power of *lashon hara*. From where [can one see]? From the spies [sent to travel through Eretz Yisrael]. If the spies, who [only] spoke derogatorily about trees and stones [were severely punished], one who speaks derogatorily about a friend is surely [subject to severe punishment].
>
> Talmud, *Arachin* 15a

---

1. *Chafetz Chaim*, Vol. I, 5:8

LASHON HARA ABOUT A SPEAKER OR LECTURER

One may not say about a speaker or lecturer:[1]

◆ "He's not worth listening to."

◆ "He doesn't know what he's talking about."

◆ "He only talks because he likes to hear himself."

Many people are not careful and make fun of the speaker after hearing a lecture. They don't realize that:

◆ They cause the lecturer embarrassment and distress, and frequently monetary loss as well.

◆ They often say their comments publicly and their sin is consequently even more serious.

◆ Generally, the quality of a lecture depends upon the listener and each person forms his own impression based on his own needs.

◆ This type of denigration usually includes exaggeration if not outright falsehood.

---

1. *Chafetz Chaim*, Vol. 1, 2:2 and note ad. loc..

LASHON HARA SPOKEN IN A PERSON'S PRESENCE OR IN HIS ABSENCE

It makes no difference if the person about whom one is speaking *lashon hara* is present or not.[1]

❖ ❖ ❖

Each of the two situations is grave for a reason that does not apply to the other.

If the person about whom one is speaking is not present:[1]

♦ then the speaker transgresses the prohibition of "cursed shall be the person who strikes his friend surreptitiously."
[*Devarim* 27:24]

If the person about whom one is speaking is present:[1]

♦ then the speaker, aside from transgressing the prohibition of *lashon hara*, is also considered to be impudent and a hatemonger.

---

1. *Chafetz Chaim*, Vol. 1, 3:1

CHAPTER 3

About whom and to whom may one not speak *Lashon Hara*

The prohibition of speaking *lashon hara* even when one is pressured to speak

> Hashem said, "if you desire to escape from [the punishment of] *gehinnom*, distance yourself from *lashon hara*, and you shall merit both this world and the world to come.
>
> *Midrash Tanchuma, Parshas Metzora*

ABOUT WHOM MAY ONE NOT SPEAK LASHON HARA

1. One may not speak *lashon hara* about an individual or a group.[1]

It is a serious sin to speak derogatorily about an entire group or community.
For example, one may not say:

♦ "All the students in the fifth grade are slow learners."

♦ "All of the residents of town x are inhospitable."

♦ "People who come from y are generally not merciful."

> And Rav Chisda said in the name of Mar Ukva: "One who speaks *lashon hara*, [about him] Hashem says, 'He and I cannot dwell [together] in the world.' As the verse (*Tehillim* 101:5) states: *For the one who speaks surreptitiously about his friend, him I shall cut off, and the one who is haughty and who has a covetous heart, him I cannot [abide]*. Read not "him" but "with him."
>
> Talmud, *Arachin* 15a

---

1. *Chafetz Chaim*, Vol. 1, 5:8

ABOUT WHOM IS IT FORBIDDEN TO SPEAK *LASHON HARA*

2. One may not speak *lashon hara* about a *talmid chacham* or about a person who is unlearned.[1]

♦ Speaking *lashon hara* about a *talmid chacham* is an extremely serious transgression and may cause spiritual damage as well, as noted on page 18.

3. One may not speak *lashon hara* about an adult or a child.[2]

♦ Speaking *lashon hara* about a child is prohibited because it may injure the child or cause him embarrassment.

---

1. *Chafetz Chaim*, Vol. I, 8:4
2. *Chafetz Chaim*, Vol. 1, 8:3. As regards speaking about children when there is a purpose, see Chapter 10.

ABOUT WHOM IS IT FORBIDDEN TO SPEAK *LASHON HARA*

4. One may not speak *lashon hara* about a person, whether he is related or not.[1]

- Speaking *lashon hara* about a relative is prohibited even though the relative does not usually mind. Moreover, even though the motive is not to denigrate the relative, but rather is an expression of a desire for truth, one is still prohibited to speak *lashon hara*.

5. One may not speak *lashon hara* about his own wife.[2]

- It is very common to fall into this kind of *Lashan Hara*; e.g., when a husband speaks to his relatives about his wife or about her family.

---

1. *Chafetz Chaim*, Vol. I, 8:1
2. *Chafetz Chaim*, Vol. 1, 8:2

THE *CHEREM* OF PREVIOUS GENERATIONS

One may not speak *lashon hara* about people who have passed away.

♦ There is an ordinance and a *cherem* (a ban that was made by the Torah Sages of previous generations) that one may not speak derogatorily about the deceased.[1]

It is even more serious to speak derogatorily about a *talmid chacham* who has passed away or to ridicule the Torah that he taught.[1]

> *For life and death are in the hands of the tongue* [*Mishlei* 18:21] — everything depends upon speech. If one is worthy, there is life. And if one is unworthy, there is death. If one used his tongue to speak words of Torah, he will merit life for the Torah is a tree of life, as the verse states: *For it is a tree of life to those who take hold of it* (Mishlei 3:18). And it is also the cure for *lashon hara*, as the verse states: *for a healing tongue is the tree of life, and one who distorts it will be broken in the wind* (Mishlei 15:4). And if one busies himself speaking *lashon hara*, he brings death upon himself, for *lashon hara* is even more serious than murder.
>
> Tanchuma, Parshas Metzora 2

---

1. *Chafetz Chaim*, Vol. 1, 8:9

TO WHOM MAY ONE NOT SPEAK *LASHON HARA*

1. One may not speak *lashon hara* to a person whether he is a relative or not.[1]

   ♦ For example, one may not inform his father that one of his brothers is acting improperly if one can achieve the same result by reproving that brother.[2]
   [However, if he has reason to believe that his reproval will have no effect, he may tell his father.]

   ♦ One may not speak *lashon hara* to his wife.[3]

> Many people fall into the trap and tell their wives all that has happened in their relationships with others. Aside from prohibition of lashon hara, doing so foments much strife. Therefore, one who is careful about his soul, should be careful not to reveal such matters to his wife.
> *Chafetz Chaim*, Vol. I, 8:1

---

1. *Chafetz Chaim*, Vol. I, 8:10
2. *Chafetz Chaim*, Vol. I, 8:11
3. *Chafetz Chaim*, Vol. I, 8:10

TO WHOM MAY ONE NOT SPEAK *LASHON HARA*

2. One may not speak *lashon hara* to a Jew and certainly not to a gentile.[1]

One who informs gentiles about the actions of a Jew is guilty of a grievous sin!

> If one informs gentiles about a Jew, without question, his sin is grievous, for by doing so, he joins the category of 'informers' whose status is equivalent to non-believers and those who deny the authority of the Torah of whom it is said, '*gehinnom* has an end but they do not'. Therefore, one should be exceedingly careful in this matter. One who transgresses and informs, is considered to have blasphemed and raised his hand to destroy the Torah given by *Moshe Rabbeinu*.
>
> *Chafetz Chaim*, Vol. I, 8:12

---

1. *Chafetz Chaim*, Vol. I, 8:12.

ONE MAY NOT SPEAK *LASHON HARA* EVEN IF PRESSURED TO DO SO

- One may not speak *lashon hara* even if others urge him to do so.[1]

- The prohibition applies even if the person urging him to speak is his father, his teacher or a king.[1]

Even if they pressure him to speak about an unrelated subject, he may not speak if, within the course of his conversation, he may come to speak *lashon hara* .

---

1. *Chafetz Chaim*, Vol. I, 1:5

THE PROHIBITION APPLIES EVEN IF BY REMAINING SILENT, PEOPLE BECOME ANGRY WITH HIM, HE IS EMBARRASSED, OR HE MAY LOSE HIS LIVELIHOOD

- One may not speak *lashon hara* even if refusing to do so causes people to become angry with him.[1]

- One may not speak *lashon hara* even if by refusing to do so people consider him to be foolish.[1]

- One may not speak *lashon hara* even if by refusing to do so he may lose his source of income.[2]

> Even if one sees that by being careful never to speak derogatorily about another Jew, he stands to suffer financial loss; e.g., in a case where he is an employee of someone else and by failing to inform on a co-worker he may lose his job, it is still prohibited to speak. This prohibition is the same as all other prohibitions —one must sacrifice all that he has rather than transgress as explained in *Yoreh Deah* 147:1.
>
> *Chafetz Chaim*, Vol. I, 1:6

---

1. *Chafetz Chaim*, Vol. I, 1:7
2. *Chafetz Chaim*, Vol. I, 1:6

IF SOMETHING IMPROPER WAS DONE AND REUVEN ASKS SHIMON, "WHO DID IT ?"

Shimon understands that Reuven suspects him. What should he say?[1]

If, through his denial, no one will know who the guilty party is, Shimon may answer, "I did not do it", without adding further details.

However, if through Shimon's denial, the guilty party will be identified:

If the action was indeed improper, Shimon may deny culpability even though by doing so, it will be understood who was guilty.

If the action is itself proper, but Reuven considers it to be improper, it is questionable as to whether Shimon may say, "I did not do it."

It is praiseworthy to go beyond the strict requirements of the law and to refrain from denying an action if, through one's denial, it is understood who did perform the action.

---

1. *Chafetz Chaim*, Vol. I, 10:17

CHAPTER 4

Lashon Hara that is true or that causes no damage

Speaking *lashon hara* that is true, or that causes no damage or that is spoken without malintent

> "*And he said, 'Indeed, the matter is known'.*" (*Shemos* 2:14).
> R. Yehuda bar Shalom said in the name of R. Chanina the Great, and the Sages said in the name of R. Alexandrai, "Moshe thought to himself and said, 'what sin has Israel committted that has brought them enslavement more severe than any other nation?' When he heard what was said [i.e, when he heard that his killing of the Egyptian had become public knowledge], he said, '*lashon hara* is [prevalent] among them. How can they be deemed worthy of redemption?' He thereupon said, 'Indeed, the matter is known; i.e., I now know the reason for their enslavement.
>
> *Shemos Rabbah* 1:35

ONE MAY NOT RELATE THE DETAILS OF AN INCIDENT EVEN IF THEY ARE TRUE

Even if all of the details of a story are true, they may not be related if they constitute *lashon hara*.[1]

One may not retell an incident even if the person speaking witnessed the incident himself.

> The story is told of a peddler who travelled through the towns in the area of Tzippori and who was wont to announce, "who wishes to purchase the elixir of life?" R. Yannai said to him, "sell it to me." The peddler took out a book of *Tehillim* and showed him the verse stating: *Who is the person who desires life (Tehillim 34:14). What is stated afterwards? Guard your tongue from evil, turn away from evil and do good.* R. Yannai said, "Shlomo also said the same thing (Mishlei 21:23): *One who guards his mouth and tongue, guards his soul from travail.*"
> *Vayikra Rabbah* 16:2

---

1. *Chafetz Chaim*, Vol. I, 1:1 and 3:3.

SPREADING AN EVIL NAME

If the *lashon hara* being recounted contains elements of falsehood, the person speaking is referred to as a

motzi shem ra

(literally, one who spreads an evil name) and his sin is considered to be very grievous.[1]

> R. Chisda said in the name of Mar Ukva, "[concerning] anyone who speaks *lashon hara*, Hashem says to the officer in charge of *gehinnom*, I shall [judge] him from above, and you shall judge him from below. As the verse states: *sharpened arrows of a brave warrior along with glowing charcoals* [*Tehillim* 120:4]. The *arrow* must refer to *lashon hara*, for the verse states: *like a drawn arrow, their tongues speak falsehood* [*Yirmiyahu* 9:7]. The *brave warrior* refers to Hashem, as the verse states: *Hashem has gone out like a brave warrior* [*Yeshayahu* 42:13]. And the glowing charcoals refer to *gehinnom*.
>
> *Arachin* 15a

---

1. *Chafetz Chaim*, Vol. I, 1:1.

ONE MAY NOT SPEAK LASHON HARA EVEN IF ONE'S INTENTION IS GOOD

♦ One may not speak *lashon hara* even if one has no intent to castigate, but rather intends to stand up for the truth.[1]

♦ Even in a situation where one is convinced that all of the necessary preconditions that would allow one to relate an incident have been fulfilled,[2] if one's judgement was mistaken and he therefore judged his friend unfavorably, he is culpable for having spoken lashon hara.[3]

> Our forefathers tested Hashem ten times and they were only punished because they spoke *lashon hara*. And [the test] of the spies [who spoke *lashon hara* about Eretz Yisroel] was the most grievous, as the verse states: *and they have tested Me ten times and have not hearkened to My voice* (Bamidbar 14).
>
> *Avos D'Rebbi Nasan*, Chapter 9

---

1. *Chafetz Chaim*, Vol. I, 5:1 and 8:1.
2. See Chapter 10.
3. *Chafetz Chaim*, Vol. I, 8:1.

SPEAKING *LASHON HARA* IS PROHIBITED EVEN IF IT CAUSES NO CASTIGATION OR DAMAGE

♦ Speech can be considered *lashon hara* and therefore prohibited, even if no damge or castigation of the subject results; e.g., if the people hearing the story do not believe it.[1]

♦ Even if the person speaking is certain that what he says will cause no harm (e.g., if he knows for certain that the story he tells will not be believed), he may still not retell the story.[1]

♦ One may not tell a derogatory story about someone else even if one has no intention of embarrassing the person and even if one is certain that the person hearing the story will not lose respect for the subject of the story.[2]

---

1. *Chafetz Chaim*, Vol. I, 3:6, and *B'eer Mayim Chayim* 3
2. *Chafetz Chaim*, Vol. I, 4 and 5:11.

IF THE PERSON HEARING THE STORY IS AWARE OF THE INCIDENT OR IF IT IS PUBLIC KNOWLEDGE

♦ One may not relate *lashon hara* even if the person listening has already heard it, and hearing it again will not cause him to further lose respect for the subject.[1]

♦ One may not relate *lashon hara* about a person, even if the incident is public knowledge, if the subject is now acting properly.[2]

> R. Shimon ben Pazi said, "the rains are only withheld because of those who speak *lashon hara*, for the verse states: *the north winds shall bring forth the rains, and an angry countenance is brought forth by hidden speech* [i.e., *lashon hara*] (*Mishlei* 25:23)."
>
> *Taanis* 7b

---

1. *Chafetz Chaim*, Vol. I, 4; *B'eer Mayim Chaim* ad. loc. 1; *ibid*. 5:11.
2. *Chafetz Chaim*, Vol. I, 2:3; *B'eer Mayim Chaim* ad. loc. 2; *ibid*. 7:13.

ONE MAY NOT RELATE *LASHON HARA* EVEN IF HE DENIGRATES HIMSELF

◆ The prohibition of *lashon hara* applies even if one includes himself in the derogatory speech.[1]

For example, one may not say, "Chaim and I are both dishonest people."

◆ Even if the person first mentions his own culpability, the speech is considered *lashon hara*.[1]

For example, one may not say, "I was at fault in the accident and so was Chaim."

◆ Even if one's purpose is to denigrate himself, and he only mentions another person to reinforce the derogatory nature of his action, the speech is considered *lashon hara*.[2]

For example, one may not say, "I convinced Chaim not to help the elderly."

---

1. *Chafetz Chaim*, Vol. I, 1:9.
2. *Chafetz Chaim*, Vol. I; *B'eer Mayim Chaim* 1:15.

LASHON HARA SPOKEN IN JEST OR INADVERTENTLY

♦ One may not speak *lashon hara* in jest, even without malice or without intent to embarrass or cause damage.[1]

♦ *Lashon hara* spoken within the context of a conversation or inadvertently is also prohibited.[2]

See Chapter 2 where we mentioned that one who speaks *lashon hara* consistently and does not even attempt to refrain from doing so is referred to as

a *baal lashon hara.*

---

1. *Chafetz Chaim*, Vol. I, 3:3.
2. *Chafetz Chaim*, Vol. I, 1:3 and 2:7.

CHAPTER 5

Lashon Hara that is not related through speech

Lashon hara by implication, in writing or in secret

> R. Shmuel bar Nachmani said: "They asked the snake, 'why are you found near fences?' He answered, ' because I breached the fence [that protected the world].' 'And why do you slither with your tongue protruding?' [The snake answered], 'it was my tongue that caused [my transgression].'"
>
> *Bamidbar Rabbah* 19:2

LASHON HARA RELATED BY IMPLICATION

Even if one does not speak derogatorily about another person, but through his gestures or facial expressions one can infer that he means to denigrate the subject being spoken about — this is considered *lashon hara*.[1]

> The Torah offers advice as to how one can avoid the prohibition of *lashon hara*: *Remember that which Hashem did unto Miriam on your way leaving Egypt*; i.e., remember consciously and verbally the gravity of the punishment that Miriam received.
>
> Though she was righteous, a prophetess, and the well gave water in her merit, and though she spoke only about her brother [Moshe] whom she loved and for whom she had endangered herself to save him, and though she did not speak derogatorily about him, but only compared him to other prophets, and though she did not speak in his presence so as not to embarrass him, and though she did not speak publicly but only to her holy brother [Aaron] in private, and though her intent was constructive and he [Moshe] was not hurt by what she said, nevertheless all of her merits did not prevent her from being punished.
>
> *Zechor L'Miriam*, Chapter 27

---

1. *Chafetz Chaim*, Vol. I, 1:8.

WRITTEN *LASHON HARA*

As noted, the prohibition of *lashon hara* is not limited to speech. Thus, writing derogatorily about someone is also considered *lashon hara*.[1]

> Shimon, his son, said, "All of my days I was raised among the wise and I found nothing more valuable than silence."
>
> *Pirkei Avos* 1:17

---

1. *Chafetz Chaim*, Vol. I, 1:8.

SHOWING CORRESPONDENCE TO A FRIEND

One may not show someone's letters or writings to another person, if the contents of the letters indicate that the writer is not smart or that he has some other failing.[1]

Doing so is considered *lashon hara* even though nothing derogatory is said about the person who wrote the letter.

> And Hashem shall be an eternal light (*Yeshayahu* 60:20). When will this occur? At the time that all of you are unified, as the verse states: you are all alive today (*Devarim* 4:4). For this is the nature of the world: If a person takes a bundle of straw, can he break them all at one time? But if he takes an individual strand — even a baby can break it. Thus you find, Israel shall only be redeemed when they are one community, as the verse states: in those days and at that time, Hashem has said, the children of Israel and the children of Yehuda will be together (*Yirmiyahu* 50:4). When they are unified — they are [worthy] of greeting the *Shechinah*.
>
> *Midrash Tanchuma, Nitzavim* 1

---

1. *Chafetz Chaim*, Vol. I, 1; *B'eer Mayim Chayim* ad. loc. 14.

SPEECH THAT CAN BE INTERPRETED EITHER DEROGATORILY OR AS A COMPLIMENT

In the case of a story that can be interpreted either derogatorily or as a compliment; if it is evident from one's tone of voice or through one's gestures that the intent is derogatory, the story is considered to be *lashon hara*.[1]

Take the following statement:
"In Reuven's house the stove is always on because they're always cooking."

The story can be interpreted derogatorily as inferring that Reuvane eats excessively. Alternatively, it can be considered to be complimentary if Reuven has a large family or owns a restaurant.

---

1. *Chafetz Chaim*, Vol. I, 3:2. See also Chapter 10.
It should be noted that this type of speech is prohibited even if the interpretation that people give falls into the category of *avak lashon hara*. See the next chapter.

LASHON HARA IN SECRET

One may not relate a story about a person, even if one does not mention the name of the person who is the subject of the story, if it is obvious from the context to whom one is referring.[1]

Even if the story itself was not derogatory, if the subject was humiliated or embarrassed by what was said, and this was the intent of the person speaking — it is considered *lashon hara*.

> Chazal referred to this type of storytelling as
> ## *lashon hara b'tzina*
> (secretive *lashon hara*)

---

1. *Chafetz Chaim*, Vol. I, 3:4.

LISTENING TO *LASHON HARA* CAN BE CONSIDERED AS HAVING SAID IT

If the person listening to *lashon hara* explicitly agrees to what was said, he is considered to have both heard and spoken *lashon hara* and his transgression is twofold.[1]

> R. Yehuda said in the name of Rav, "when David said to Mepiboshes: *you and Tziva shall share the field (Shmuel II 19:30)*, a Heavenly voice came forth and said, 'Rechavam and Yeravam shall share the kingdom'." R. Yehuda said in the name of Rav, "had David not listened to *lashon hara*, the kingdom of the House of David would not have been divided and Israel would not have worshipped false gods [for when the kingdom was split, Yeravam set up calves for the people to worship so that they would refrain from ascending to Jerusalem where Rechavam reigned] and we would not have been exiled from our land."
>
> *Shabbos 56b*

---

1. *Chafetz Chaim*, Vol. I, 6:1.

CHAPTER 6

*Avak Lashon Hara**

Forms of speech that are Rabbinically proscribed

> R. Yochanan said in the name of R. Yosi ben Zimra, "what is the meaning of the verse, '*What will you receive and how will you benefit from deceitful speech*' (Psalms 120:3)? Hashem said to the tongue, 'all of man's organs stand erect while you lay flat, all man's organs are external while you are internal. Moreover, I have surrounded you with two walls, one of bone (the teeth) and one of flesh. *What will you receive and how will you benefit* (i.e., what more can Hashem give you to protect you) *from deceitful speech?*'"
>
> *Arachin 15b*

---

* The term *Avak Lashon Hara* is best translated as traces of *lashon hara*. For the sake of simplicity, we have chosen to transliterate the Hebrew term rather than use the translation.

AVAK LASHON HARA

Avak lashon hara refers to those forms of speech that are Rabbinically proscribed.

These forms include:

♦ Speech which can lead others to speak *lashon hara*.

♦ Speech whose contents can lead someone to infer that a person acted reprehensibly although no specific details are mentioned.

♦ Speech which is laudatory but is, nevertheless, damaging.

♦ Speech which can lead those listening to assume that *lashon hara* is being related.

AVAK LASHON HARA

1. One may not say things which may lead others to speak *lashon hara*.

♦ For example, one may not praise someone in the presence of that person's enemy or in the presence of a person whom one has reason to assume is angry with the subject of the praise.[1]

♦ Additionally, one may not praise someone publicly unless he is certain that those listening will not castigate the person about whom he is speaking.[2]

> The proscription of *avak lashon hara* applies even though the person speaking did not himself say anything derogatory.
>
> Moreover, the speaker transgresses the prohibition even if those listening would have spoken *lashon hara* regardless of what he had said.
>
> If the speaker causes others to speak *lashon hara*, he is also culpable for having transgressed the Torah prohibition of *"you shall not place a stumbling block in front of the blind"*.

---

1. *Chafetz Chaim*, Vol. I, 9:1.
It should be noted. however, that if the subject of the conversation is widely known as being worthy and righteous, he may be praised even in the presence of an enemy.
2. *Chafetz Chaim*, Vol. I, 9:2.

AVAK LASHON HARA

2. One may not say things which can lead others to speak *lashon hara*.

♦ One may not praise someone profusely.[1]

♦ This pertains even when no one present bears the subject ill will or even if the praise is not said publicly.

♦ The very fact that the subject is praised profusely may lead someone listening — or even the speaker himself — to qualify the praise in some derogatory fashion.

> Hashem said: "Because speakers of *lashon hara* were prevalent, I withdrew the Divine Presence from their midst in this world. As the verse states: *for Hashem has been uplifted into the heavens* (Psalms 57:6). However, in the world to come, when I [Hashem] will remove *lashon hara* from among you, as the verse states: *and I shall remove the hearts of stone from your flesh* (Yechezkel 36:26), I shall return My Divine Presence to rest upon you. You shall all be worthy of Torah and shall dwell in peace in the world."
>
> *Devarim Rabbah* 6:

---

1. *Chafetz Chaim*, Vol. I, 9:1.

AVAK LASHON HARA

3. One may not ask questions that can lead the respondent to speak *lashon hara*.

One should be careful, for example, not to ask someone how he fared in court. If he was found culpable, the question may cause him to speak derogatorily about the judges or rabbi who dealt with his case.[1]

> Daily life is replete with such situations. Therefore, when asking for details about something that has transpired, one should be exceedingly careful and refrain from asking questions if the answers may cause the respondent to speak *lashon hara*.

---

1. *Chafetz Chaim*, Vol. I, 9; *B'eer Mayim Chaim* ad. loc. 4.

AVAK LASHON HARA

4. One may not say things whose contents can lead someone to infer that a person acted reprehensibly even if no specific details are mentioned.

For example, one should not say:

♦ "Whoever would have thought that Reuven would end up like this."[1]

♦ "I can't tell you what happened to Reuven."[1]

♦ "I don't want to speak *lashon hara* about Reuven."

> As we noted in the previous chapter, *lashon hara* through hints or even inferences drawn from hand motions, is considered to fall into the category of speech that the Torah forbids.[2]

---

1. *Chafetz Chaim*, Vol. I, 9:1
2. *Chafetz Chaim*, Vol. I, 9; *B'eer Mayim Chaim* ad. loc. 2.

AVAK LASHON HARA

5. One should not praise a person in a manner that might cause him monetary loss.

For example:
♦ One should not publicize his host's generosity and expand upon the trouble that the host took on his behalf or how gracious he was.[1] Such speech may cause less responsible people to take advantage of the host.[1]

♦ One should not publicize that he was granted a loan by someone. Doing so may cause others — who are less trustworthy — to approach that person for help and he might feel unable to refuse them.[1]

> Regarding one who publicizes a person who has done him a favor, the verse states: *He who praises his friend loudly in the early morning, is considered to have cursed him* (Mishlei 27:14).

---

1. *Chafetz Chaim*, Vol. I, 9:3.

AVAK LASHON HARA

6. One should be careful not to speak in a manner which can cause others to assume that he is speaking *lashon hara*.[1]

For example:

♦ One is speaking *lashon hara* which is permitted because it is considered to be beneficial (as we shall see in Chapter 9), but he does not inform those listenering that his intent is beneficial.

♦ One is speaking *lashon hara* which is considered beneficial, but those listening do not believe that his intent is beneficial.

> One who does whatever possible to guard his tongue and exhorts others to be careful in this regard so as to insure that Hashem's *mitzvos* and Torah are not, G-d forbid, ignored, is deemed most worthy. In truth, all of Israel is considered to be righteous and upright. However, because of lack of knowledge of the laws concerning this, and because many are unaware of the means through which they can avoid the urge to speak *lashon hara*, the *mitzvah* of guarding one's tongue is not widely observed. One who takes it upon himself to exhort them to be more careful shall surely receive great reward, and the merit of the community will be considered to be dependent upon him.
>
> *Shmiras Halashon*, end of Volume One.

---

1. *Chafetz Chaim*, Vol. I, 9:3.

CHAPTER 7

Accepting *Lashon Hara* and the obligation to judge favorably

Accepting *Lashon Hara* and the obligation to judge favorably

> R. Yochanan said: Why was Yeravam ben Yoash, King of Israel, counted as one of the kings of Yehuda? Because he did not accept *lashon hara* [spoken about] Amos. The verse states: And Amatzyah, the *kohen* of Beis El, sent [a message] to Yeravam, the King of Israel, stating, "Amos has fomented a plot against you among the people of Israel and the land cannot contain all of his words, for thus has Amos said, 'Yeravam shall die by the sword and Israel shall be exiled from its land'." [Yeravam] responded: "Heaven forbid. That righteous man has not spoken in this manner, and if he did, what can I do to him for Hashem has told him."
>
> *Pesachim 87b*

WHAT CONSTITUTES ACCEPTING *LASHON HARA*

One may not accept the *lashon hara* that he hears as being true, for by doing so, one will lose respect for the person who is the subject of the conversation.[1]

Moreover, even if he already knows that what is being said is true, if he loses respect for the subject of the conversation as a result of what is being said, the speech is forbidden as *lashon hara*.[2]

---

1. *Chafetz Chaim*, Vol. I, 6.
If the person listening shows his acceptance of what is being said openly (through a gesture or hand motion), he is doubly culpable: 1] for having accepted *lashon hara* and 2] for having spoken it.
2. *Chafetz Chaim*, Vol. I, 8:7; *B'eer Mayim Chaim* ad. loc. 24. Vol. I, 7:7-8 outlines the details of the laws pertaining to the acceptance of *lashon hara* spoken by someone who has the credence of two witnesses. In subheading 9, the author discusses the laws pertaining to accepting *lashon hara* spoken by someone in the course of a conversation. Subheadings 10-12 outline the laws pertaining to accepting *lashon hara* when the details of the conversation lend credibility to what is being said. The *halachic* limitations outlined there, and in *B'eer Mayim Chaim* ad. loc., indicate that there is almost no situation where it is permissible to accept *lashon hara*.

JUDGING PEOPLE FAVORABLY

◆ *You shall judge your fellow man favorably* (*Vayikra* 19:15) This verse teaches us the obligation to judge people favorably.[1]

◆ If the subject of the conversation is a G-d fearing man, and more so if the *lashon hara* is being told about a *talmid chacham*, the requirement to judge favorably is even greater.[2]

> Judging favorably includes any and all means through which one can mitigate the severity of the derogatory speech; e.g., that the subject had no intention of doing something wrong, that he was unaware that the action that he did was prohibited, or that some of the details of the action are unknown (for often, forgotten details can change the entire picture).

---

1. *Chafetz Chaim*, Vol. I, 6:7.
2. *Chafetz Chaim*, Vol. I, 6:8.

JUDGING FAVORABLY WHEN THE STORY IS TRUE

♦ The obligation to judge favorably applies even in a situation where one knows that what is being said is true.[1]

♦ If it was possible to judge the subject favorably, and one failed to do so, he transgresses the following prohibitions:
You shall judge your fellow man favorably.
The prohibition of accepting *lashon hara*, for by accepting what was said, he has lost respect for the person being spoken about.

---

1. *Chafetz Chaim*, Vol. I, 6:7.
If it is possible to judge the subject favorably, there is no obligation to assume that what was said was untrue. The prohibition of accepting *lashon hara* as true applies only if he loses respect for the subject as a result of what he heard. Thus, if he does not lose respect for the subject — because he was able to judge him favorably — no prohibition would apply. See *Chafetz Chaim*, Vol. I, 6 and *B'eer Mayim Chaim*, subheading 1.

THE OBLIGATION OF JUDGING PEOPLE FAVORABLY

If one saw someone doing something that is prohibited (even if he saw that person doing so repeatedly):
If that person is usually careful not to act in a prohibited manner, he may not reveal what he saw, nor may he hate the person, and he must judge him favorably.[1]

The means through which he can judge him favorably are:
♦ He should assume that the person did not know that the specific action was prohibited.
♦ He should assume that the person thought that the prohibition was a voluntary stringency.
♦ He should assume that the person had no intention of doing the action.

> When Yeshayah said, *for I am a man of impure lips and I dwell among an impure people* (Yeshayah 6:6), Hashem said to him, "Yeshayah, you are permitted to say *I am a man of impure lips* about yourself, but about Israel you say *and I dwell among an impure people*?!" The verse says [concerning Yeshayah's statement]: *and one of the Seraphim came upon me and in his hand was a burning coal.* What is meant by a burning coal? A burning coal [to be thrown] on he who speaks *lashon hara* about my child.
>
> *Midrash Tanchuma, Vayishlach*

---

1. *Chafetz Chaim*, Vol. I, 4:3.

JUDGING FAVORABLY IN CASES WHERE CIRCUMSTANCES INDICATE THAT THERE ARE ALMOST NO GROUNDS TO DO SO

♦ If the circumstances concern a person who is usually careful to refrain from acting improperly, one should treat the matter as being doubtful (rather than assume that the action was improper).[1]

♦ If the circumstances concern a *talmid chacham*, one is obligated to judge him favorably.[2]

If there is no means of judging him favorably,[3] e.g., if it is clear that the person knew that the action was prohibited and it is obvious that he acted intentionally:

If the person only acted improperly once in private, one may not reveal what he has done, one may not embarrass him and one is obligated to offer reproval.

---

1. *Chafetz Chaim*, Vol. I, 3:7.
2. *Chafetz Chaim*, Vol. I, 4:4.
3. See *Chafetz Chaim*, Vol. I, 4 regarding the following:
a) if the person is known as one who does not refrain from acting improperly.
b) if the person does not accept reproof.
c) if the person does not fear G-d.
d) if the person is considered to be wicked (and is therefore no longer considered to be one's fellow Jew).

WHAT TYPES OF INFORMATION MAY ONE NOT ACCEPT

♦ Any speech which falls into the category of being forbidden, may not be accepted.[1]

This includes:
Any topic about which one may not speak because of the prohibition of *lashon hara*.[2]
Any form of speech that is prohibited as *lashon hara*; e.g., through gestures rather than through speech.[3]

♦ Under certain circumstances, the prohibition of accepting *lashon hara* may apply even though the person speaking is himself not culpable; e.g., when he is relating *lashon hara* for a permissible purpose.[4]

In this situation, the person listening should not accept the *lashon hara* as true but should rather treat what is being said as a warning to be careful when dealing with the subject.[5]

---

1. *Chafetz Chaim*, Vol. I, 6:9.
2. See Chapter 1.
3. See Chapter 5.
4. See *Chafetz Chaim*, Vol. I, 6; *B'eer Mayim Chaim*, subheading 24.
5. See Chapter 9.

IF TWO PEOPLE RELATE THE INCIDENT OR IF THE PERSON SPEAKING IS ESPECIALLY RELIABLE

One may not accept *lashon hara*:
♦ Even if the incident is related by two or more people.[1]
♦ Even if the person speaking is especially reliable; e.g., one's father, mother or close relative.[2]

> Resh Lakish said: what is the meaning of the verse, *can the serpent strike without a whisper, and there is no benefit to he who can speak (Koheleth 10:11)*. In the time to come, all of the animals shall gather and shall approach the serpent and say to him: "The lion preys and eats, the wolf attacks and eats, but what enjoyment do you have?" The serpent shall respond: *what benefit is there to one who speaks (lashon hara)*.
>
> *Ta'anis 8a*

---
1. *Chafetz Chaim*, Vol. I, 7:3.
2. *Chafetz Chaim*, Vol. I, 8:14.

WHEN A MATTER IS PUBLIC KNOWLEDGE OR WHEN THE SPEAKER CASTIGATES HIMSELF AS WELL

One may not accept *lashon hara*:

♦ Even if the incident is related in the presence of many people.[1]

♦ Even if the incident was printed and publicized.[2]

♦ Even if the incident is known to all.[3]

♦ Even if the person relating the incident includes himself as being culpable.[4]

---

1. *Chafetz Chaim*, Vol. I, 7:1.
2. See *Chafetz Chaim*, Vol. I, 7:10; *B'eer Mayim Chaim* ad. loc. 24. One may not accept the *lashon hara* since one is required to judge favorably.
3. See *Chafetz Chaim*, Vol. I, 7:4 for details.
4. *Chafetz Chaim*, Vol. I, 7:6. In this case, the listener may believe those details that the speaker relates about himself but may not accept that which is said about others.

ACCEPTING *LASHON HARA* SPOKEN IN THE PRESENCE OF THE SUBJECT

One may not accept *lashon hara*:
- Even if the person speaking says that he is willing to relate the incident in the presence of the subject.[1]
- Even if he relates the incident in the subject's presence.
- Even if the subject does not deny the incident.[1]

Even if the subject is not the type of person who usually refrains from responding to accusations, his silence cannot be taken to be corroboration and one is not permitted to believe the *lashon hara*.[1]

> All coals are extinguished from within, but broom embers — though extinguished on the outside — still burn from within. Similarly, anyone who accepts *lashon hara* (concerning another person); though one may assuage the subject and he appears to accept what is said, he still burns within (because of what was said). It once happened that a broom was set afire, and it burned for eighteen months.
>
> *Bereishis Rabbah* 98:23

---

1. *Chafetz Chaim*, Vol. I, 7:2.

CONCERNING WHOM MAY ONE NOT ACCEPT *LASHON HARA*

A Jew may not accept *lashon hara* that relates to his fellow Jew[1] (unless that person is no longer considered to be his fellow Jew).

> *Sharpened arrows of a brave warrior* (*Tehillim* 120:4). Why did he [Dovid *Hamelech*] see fit to compare them (i.e., *lashon hara*) to arrows rather than to other implements of warfare? Other implements of warfare strike from close up, whereas the arrow strikes from afar. The same is true of *lashon hara*. That which is said in Rome kills in Syria.
>
> *Bereishis Rabbah* 98:23

---

1. *Chafetz Chaim*, Vol. I,8:13. As regards accepting *lashon hara* about those who are no longer considered to be one's fellow Jew (e.g., *apikorsim* or informers), see 7:5-6. The laws regarding accepting *lashon hara* about people who contemptuosly transgress prohibitions that all are aware of, are outlined in 8:7. See also 6 and *B'eer Mayim Chaim*, ad. loc. 26. The laws regarding acceptance of *lashon hara* about those who constantly foment strife are outlined in 8:8.

CHAPTER 8

Listening to *Lashon Hara*

The prohibition of listening to *lashon hara* and the laws pertaining to *lashon hara* spoken for a purpose

> "My son, do not sit in the company of those who speak badly about their friends, for when their words ascend, they are recorded, and all those who were part of the group [who heard what was said] are recorded as being members of an evil group and as *baalei lashon hara*.
>
> *Pirkei D'Rebbi Eliezer*

THE PROHIBITION OF LISTENING TO *LASHON HARA*

The Torah prohibits listening to *lashon hara* even if one has no intention of accepting or believing what is said.[1]

> It is known that Hashem promised that He would not enter the heavenly Beth HaMikdash until Israel built the Beth HaMikdash on earth. As long as we do not rectify our actions and thus, the earthly Beth HaMikdash cannot be built, Hashem cannot enter the heavenly Beth HaMikdash. Thus, we shall be presented with the following question. Why are you the last to return the King of Kings to His home? Although, ultimately, the matter shall be resolved even without our assistance, why should we be the cause for the long delay. Each day that we are negligent about rectifying our actions causes this question to be posed.
>
> Therefore, each one of us should make haste to root out purposeless hate and the sin of *lashon hara*, for then the King shall be able to immediately re-enter His home. All who hasten to correct this matter shall be worthy of great merit.
>
> *Kuntres Kavod Shamayim*, Chapter III

---

1. *Chafetz Chaim* Vol. I, 6:2

LISTENING TO *LASHON HARA* FOR A PURPOSE

♦ One may listen to *lashon hara* if one does so for a beneficial purpose in the future.[1]

♦ However, though one may listen to what is being said, one may only accept what is related as a basis for being wary of the subject. One may not accept what is said as being factual as will be explained.[2]

♦ One may make inquiries regarding a person and his actions when one does so for a purpose. However, one must make it clear that the inquiries are being made for a purpose rather than out of curiosity.[3]

---

1. See the next chapter.
2. *Chafetz Chaim* Vol. I, 6:2
3. Chapter 16 outlines the *halachic* guidelines that one must follow when making inquiries.

FOR WHAT PURPOSE MAY ONE LISTEN TO *LASHON HARA*

♦ One may listen to *lashon hara* if one has a specific future purpose; e.g., to prevent damage, to return stolen items, or to warn someone to stay away from an unscrupulous person.[1]

♦ Additionally, one may listen to *lashon hara* even if his purpose is to benefit others rather than himself.[1]

♦ One may also listen to *lashon hara* if by so doing, one can help the person speaking judge the subject of the conversation favorably, or calm the speaker so that he refrains from speaking about the subject to others.[2]

---

1. *Chafetz Chaim* Vol. I, 6:2
2. *Chafetz Chaim* Vol. I, 6:4

ONE MAY NOT CAUSE THE SPEAKER TO TRANSGRESS

♦ One may listen to *lashon hara* for a purpose, provided that the person speaking also has a purpose in relating the *lashon hara*. If the speaker has no such intention, by listening, one causes the speaker to transgress.[1]

♦ However, if the person was already speaking, one may listen — provided that one has a purpose in doing so. Though the speaker is guilty of having spoken *lashon hara*, the listener is not the one who caused him to speak.[2]

---

1. *Chafetz Chaim* Vol. I, 6:2
2. *Chafetz Chaim* Vol. I, 6:2; *B'eer Mayim Chayim* 3

ONE MAY NOT ACCEPT THE *LASHON HARA* EVEN IN SITUATIONS WHEN ONE IS PERMITTED TO LISTEN

♦ One should be extremely careful not to accept what he hears as being factual. Rather, one should use what is being said as a basis for being wary of the subject; e.g., to prevent being hurt by the person under discussion.[1]

♦ Moreover, one should not even accept what is said as being a possibility. Every person is assumed to be righteous and one may not abrogate this assumption without concrete evidence.[2]

---

1. *Chafetz Chaim* Vol. I, 6:4
2. *Chafetz Chaim* Vol. I, 6:10

ONE MAY NOT ACCEPT THE *LASHON HARA* EVEN IN SITUATIONS WHEN ONE IS PERMITTED TO LISTEN

♦ Though one may listen and be wary, one may not use what is said as a basis for acting against the subject.
For example:
   One may not hurt or embarrass the subject.
   One may not hate him even secretly.

♦ One must continue to deal with the subject righteously and perform all of the acts of kindness and *tzedakah* for him that the Torah requires.[1]

> At the time of *krias shema*, when one recites the verse *and you shall place these things in your heart* which alludes to the acceptance of the yoke of heaven, one should accept upon himself not to transgress the negative and positive commandments that are dependent upon speech.
>
> *Chovas Hashmirah,* Chapter 10

---

1. *Chafetz Chaim* Vol. I, 6:11

CHAPTER 9

Lashon Hara spoken for a purpose

Under which circumstances may one speak *lashon hara* for a purpose

> Upon consideration, we find that the fulfillment of the obligation to judge people favorably and the obligation to guard one's tongue, are dependent upon the *mitzvah* of "loving one's neighbor as oneself". If one truly loves his neighbor, he will surely refrain from speaking *lashon hara* about him and he will do his utmost to find grounds to judge him favorably.
>
> *Shmiras Halashon, Sha'ar Hatevunah*

SPEAKING *LASHON HARA* FOR A PURPOSE WHEN THE SUBJECT IS A PERSON WHO HAS DONE SOMETHING WRONG

If one saw a person acting badly (e.g., if he saw him stealing or causing damage or embarrassment) and he is certain that the action has not been rectified (e.g., the stolen property was not returned or the damage was not paid for), one may relate what he witnessed provided that the following conditions are met:[1]

> 1 - The person speaking must be completely certain of the truth.
>
> 2 - He must be sure that the act is indeed considered to be wrong according to the Torah.
>
> 3 - He must first rebuke the person if there is a possibility that the person will accept his reproval.[2]

☞

---

1. See *Chafetz Chaim* Vol. I, 10:2 and *B'eer Mayim Chayim* ad. loc.
2. If the subject is a person who will not tolerate rebuke, the incident should be related in the presence of three people. If he is afraid of the subject, he may relate the incident to one person. If the speaker is considered to be a credible person, and has a reputation of not being afraid of others. then the incident may be related to one person.

SPEAKING *LASHON HARA* FOR A PURPOSE WHEN THE SUBJECT IS A PERSON WHO HAS DONE SOMETHING WRONG

4 - When relating the incident, he must make sure that he is doing so for a purpose rather than out of hatred.

5 - If it is possible to accomplish the purpose through other means, one may not relate the incident.

6 - One must be careful not to cause the subject greater damage than he is liable for according to law.

7 - One may not exaggerate the incident. By doing so, one is considered to be a *motzi shem ra* (a person who spreads bad names).[3]

---

3. The laws of speaking *lashon hara* about people who cause strife, are brought in *Chafetz Chaim* Vol. I, 8:8 and *B'eer Mayim Chayim* ad. loc.

SPEAKING *LASHON HARA* FOR A PURPOSE

Even the person who was himself wronged is permitted to relate what transpired to people who have influence on the person who committed the act.[1]

♦ Relating what transpired can be considered a valid purpose since those people will rebuke the subject and might even influence him to rectify the action (e.g., by returning the stolen item).

♦ It is praiseworthy to downplay the severity of the action, if the desired purpose can still be accomplished.[2]

♦ It should be noted that when speaking, one must be careful to fulfill the conditions outlined on the previous pages.

---

1. *Chafetz Chaim* Vol. I, 10:13
2. *Chafetz Chaim* Vol. I, 10:14

SPEAKING *LASHON HARA* FOR A CONSTRUCTIVE PURPOSE

One may relate *lashon hara* so as to prevent the subject from causing him harm in the future, provided that the previously outlined conditions are met.

If recounting the incident enables the victim to stop worrying that the person who harmed him may do so again, it is possible that this too can be considered to be a valid purpose — provided that the conditions already outlined are met.[1]

> R. Elazar said in the name of R. Yosi ben Zimra: Man has 248 limbs, some of which are upright and some of which are prone. His tongue is encased between two cheeks, his saliva runs below it and the tongue itself is folded and refolded. Yet come and see how many conflagurations it [the tongue] causes. Were it upright, it would surely be so [i.e., it would be able to cause even more damage]. Therefore, Moshe warns Israel and tells them, this is the law of the *metzora*, [i.e., read the word *metzora* as if were written] *motzi ra* [i.e., a person who speaks *lashon hara* about others].
>
> *Vayikra Rabba,* 16:4

---

1. *Chafetz Chaim* Vol. I, 10:13-14

ONE MAY WARN OTHERS NOT TO ASSOCIATE WITH UNSAVORY PEOPLE

It is a *mitzvah* to warn one's children and students to refrain from associating with people who may have bad influence on them.

The following conditions apply:[1]

♦ One's motivation must be to accomplish a purpose rather than be generated out of hatred.

♦ One may not classify those spoken about as being evil for it is possible that they may have changed their ways or that they may be unaware of the severity of their actions.

♦ One must be careful in relating the matter. One may only say "I saw X do something" if he actually witnessed what transpired. If he only heard of what happened, he must be careful to say, "I heard."

♦ The person speaking must make it clear that his only motivation is to accomplish a specific purpose. Otherwise, those listening may assume that he is speaking *lashon hara* and may themselves learn from his actions and assume that one may speak about others.

---

1. See *Chafetz Chaim* Vol. I, 4:10 and *B'eer Mayim Chayim* ad. loc.

ONE MAY WARN OTHERS NOT TO ASSOCIATE WITH UNSAVORY PEOPLE

There are many situations in which it is a *mitzvah* to warn others about unsavory people.[1]

When doing so, one must be careful to fulfill the conditions that were previously outlined.

For example:
♦ If someone is about to extend credit to a person from whom it will be difficult to collect, one may warn the seller or lender to exercise caution. However, if one only heard that the person is a credit risk, he should emphasize when speaking that his information is based on hearsay.

♦ One may tell someone "X claims that you stole a certain object" so that the person will be careful to save his receipt or proof of purchase in order to be able to prove that he did not steal the object.

---

1. *Chafetz Chaim* Vol. I, 4:10 and *B'eer Mayim Chaim* ad. loc.

SPEAKING *LASHON HARA* ABOUT A CHILD

♦ One may not relate an incident that concerns the actions of a child unless one does so to accomplish a beneficial purpose.[1]

♦ If the purpose is to have those listening give the child direction or to prevent the child's actions from causing damage, one may relate the incident.

The following conditions must be met:

1. One must be certain that he has all of the facts.

2. One should not rely solely on information provided by others.

The person speaking should take into account the ramifications of relating the incident in order to ensure that as a result of what he is says, the child does not suffer punishment that is unfair.

---

1. *Chafetz Chaim* Vol. I, 8:3; *B'eer Mayim Chaim* ad. loc. 7

CHAPTER 10

Lashon Hara spoken in front of three people or in the subject's presence

---

Lashon Hara spoken in front of three people or in the subject's presence
Revealing a Secret

> One who wishes to heal his tongue, should partake from the "tree of life" — the Torah — for by eating from it, one can earn eternal life. Know that the study of Torah is the means through which one can avoid *lashon hara*.
>
> *Shmiras Halashon, Sha'ar Hatorah* 1

SUBJECTS WHICH MAY BE RELATED IN THE PRESENCE OF THREE PEOPLE

Subjects which are not entirely derogatory; i.e., if they can be interpreted as either complimentary or critical depending upon the intonations or expressions of the person speaking, may be related in the presence of three people. The reason why it is permitted is because the person speaking in front of three people knows that what he says will be repeated to others. Therefore, he will be careful when speaking to insure that what he says should not be interpreted unfavorably.[1]

> For example, take the following statement: "You'll be able to find a lit fire in Reuven's house because they're always cooking."
> The statement can be taken as being critical of Reuven if the person listening assumes that Reuven has many parties et. al.
> On the other hand, it can also be taken as being a statement of fact without any implied criticism if Reuven has a large household or many guests.

---

1. *Chafetz Chaim* Vol. I, 8:2; see *B'eer Mayim Chaim* ad. loc. 2,3. If there are less than three people present, one should refrain from making this kind of statement since he will not exercise caution when speaking to insure that those listening not infer that he means to be critical of Reuven.

LASHON HARA SPOKEN IN FRONT OF THREE PEOPLE

Subjects which have derogatory implications, may not be related even if three people are present.[1]

The prohibition applies even if the subject is not entirely derogatory; e.g., if the person about whom one is speaking has done something which is considered wrong although it is not forbidden.

> Resh Lakish said, he who speaks *lashon hara* increases his sins until they reach heaven for the verse states: *they direct their tongues against heaven and their tongues walk on earth* (Tehillim 73:9).
>
> Arachin 15b

---

1. *Chafetz Chaim* Vol. I, 2:2.

LASHON HARA SPOKEN IN THE SUBJECT'S PRESENCE

One may relate an incident which can be interpreted as being either complimentary or critical depending upon the intonation or expression of the speaker, provided that one would not be embarrassed to do so if the subject were present.[1]

This type of speech is permitted because the fact that he would not hesitate to speak even if the subject were present indicates that he has no intention of being critical. Hence, even if the subject is not present, he may relate the incident.

If, however, it is obvious from his expression or intonation that he intends to be critical, one may not relate the incident even if the speech is considered to be *avak lashon hara*.

---

1. *Chafetz Chaim* Vol. I, 3:2.

MAY ONE RETELL *LASHON HARA* THAT HE HEARD SPOKEN IN THE PRESENCE OF THREE PEOPLE?

◆ If a person transgressed, and spoke *lashon hara* in front of three people, those who heard are duty bound not to accept or believe what was said.

◆ However, if one of the three repeated what was said under the terms of the conditions that are outlined on the following pages, some authorities maintain that he would not be considered culpable for having spoken *lashon hara*.[1] Since what was said will eventually become public knowledge, the Torah did not prohibit this type of speech. It should be noted that there are authorities who maintain that this type of speech is prohibited since we do not find grounds in the Talmud to permit it.

◆ This applies only in a situation where three people heard what was said. If two people repeated the conversation to another two people, the prohibition of *lashon hara* applies.

◆ Derogatory remarks about a person's ancestors or about a person's previous actions, may not be said even if they had previously been retold before three people.

---

1. *Chafetz Chaim* Vol. I, 2:3-10, *B'eer Mayim Chaim* ad. loc.

MAY ONE RETELL *LASHON HARA* THAT HE HEARD SPOKEN IN THE PRESENCE OF THREE PEOPLE ?

All of the following conditions must be met before one may relate an incident that he heard spoken in front of three people.

1 - The person speaking must have himself heard the incident spoken about in the presence of three people.

2 - If one of the three people who were present when the incident was related is especially G-d fearing and is known as one who refrains from speaking *lashon hara*, or possibly, if one of the three is a relative or close friend of the subject of the conversation, the incident may not be related. As we previously noted, incidents that are retold in front of three may be retold since they become public knowledge. However, since one of the three who heard the conversation is either G-d fearing or a close friend or relative of the subject, it is possible that the incident will not become public knowledge since he would not retell it to others.

3 - When relating the incident, one may only do so within the course of a conversation and without intending to publicize the incident. Some authorities maintain that if the incident is the only topic of the conversation, one may not relate it.

MAY ONE RETELL *LASHON HARA* THAT HE HEARD SPOKEN IN THE PRESENCE OF THREE PEOPLE ?

4 - One may not add any details that were not part of the original conversation.

5 - One may only retell the incident in a place where it is conceivable that people will have heard about the incident from one of the three people who were originally present.

6 - If the person listening accepts and believes *lashon hara*, one may not relate the incident to him.

7 - If the person who originally recounted the incident warned the listeners not to reveal what he said, one may not retell the incident.

As can be seen, it is almost impossible for all of these conditions to be met. Moreover, even if all of the conditions are met, some authorities maintain that the incident may still not be related.

REVEALING A SECRET

If a person related something to another person, that person may not reveal what was said to others unless the person who told him gave him permission to do so, and provided that what was said is not *lashon hara*.[1]

> There was a student who revealed, after twenty-two years, something (*lashon hara*) that was said in the study hall. R. Ami banished him from the study hall and said of him: He reveals secrets.
>
> *Sanhedrin* 31a

---

1. *Chafetz Chaim* Vol. I, 9:6.

REVEALING A PERSON'S SECRETS

◆ If someone told another person a secret that concerned himself, and publicizing what was told will not cause that person any pain or damage, one may reveal the secret to others even though it was not told in the presence of three people.[1]

◆ It is considered praiseworthy not to reveal anything that others told one unless one was given permission.[1]

◆ Perhaps, it depends upon how the person related the incident or matter. If it is obvious that the person does not want the matter to be publicized; e.g., if he related it privately, then it is forbidden to reveal it to others. If that person, however, did not show that he wishes the mater to remain secret, it it permissible to reveal it.[1]

---

1. *Chafetz Chaim* Vol. I, 8:2; *B'eer Mayim Chaim* ad. loc. 27.

REVEALING A PERSON'S SECRETS

If someone revealed personal information about himself that, if publicized, could cause damage or pain to him, one may not reveal the information to others.[1]

However, if he revealed the matter in front of three people, it is obvious that he is not worried about the matter becoming public knowledge. Consequently, one may reveal what was said, provided that the following conditions are met.

1 - Only the person who actually heard from the person who revealed the secret may retell it. Others, who heard the secret second-hand, may not retell the incident.

2 - The two other people who heard the secret from the person must also be in a position to retell it.

3 - One may not add additional details.

4 - One may only retell the incident in a place where it would become known even if he did not retell it.

---

1. See *Chafetz Chaim* Vol. I, 2:13 and *B'eer Mayim Chaim* ad. loc. 28.

REVEALING A PERSON'S SECRETS

5 - If the person who hears him tell the secret accepts it as fact, one may not retell it.

6 - If the person told the three people not to reveal it to others, the secret may not be retold.

One need not be particular to fulfill the condition that the incident be retold inobtrusively in the course of the conversation. However, if the secret is potentially embarrassing or damaging — e.g., if the person revealed that he had done something wrong — one should be careful to retell the information only in an incidental manner.

CHAPTER 11

Avoiding and repenting for the sin of *Lashon Hara*

> The holy works record that there are four periods for repenting. 1] The optimum time is to repent daily before retiring for then the sin will not have yet been recorded. 2] On *Erev Shabbos*. 3] On *Erev Rosh Chodesh*. 4] On *Erev Yom Kippur*. One must search inside himself to see whether he acted properly regarding his speech. If he finds that he has not stumbled, it is right that he record in his own notebook that G-d has helped him and he should be happy that this is his lot. He should offer thanks to G-d for what has transpired and he should ask for further help in the future. He should always bear in mind that which our sages said. "Hashem says, 'My son, if you wish to save yourself from Gehinnom — be careful to avoid *lashon hara* (which includes all manners of forbidden speech).'" He should also avoid searching for lenient rulings regarding *lashon hara* and should make every possible effort to avoid being ensnared by the trap of this inclination.
>
> *Zechor L'Miriam*, Chapter 25

JOINING A GROUP OF PEOPLE WHO ARE SPEAKING *LASHON HARA*

One transgresses the prohibition of *lashon hara* if one joins a group of people who are *baalei lashon hara* and:

◆ they had been speaking *lashon hara* before he joined them.

◆ if he can leave the group but does not do so.

◆ if he knows that they are the type of people who speak *lashon hara* and does not refrain from joining the group (even though they have not as yet spoken lashon hara).

In all of these cases, he is considered to be as culpable as they are.[1]

---

1. Chafetz Chaim Vol. I, 6:6.

WHAT SHOULD ONE DO IF HE FINDS HIMSELF IN A GROUP SPEAKING *LASHON HARA*?

If one is sitting with a group of people, and they begin to speak *lashon hara*, the following actions should be taken:[1]

◆ One should attempt to reprove them even if he has reason to assume that it will have no effect, provided that the reproval itself will not cause even more harm.

◆ If he has reason to believe that his reproval will cause harm (e.g., if as a result of his reproval the group will speak even more *lashon hara*), one should not reprove them but should rather do his best to change the subject of the conversation.

◆ If he is unsuccessful in changing the subject, he is required to get up and leave or to stop listening.

◆ If he cannot leave and he finds that he cannot help but listen, he should at least try the following three things so as to avoid transgressing the Torah prohibition of listening to *lashon hara*:
 a] he should decide that he will not accept or believe what is being said.
 b] he should show his dissatisfaction with what is being said.
 c] he should offer no signs that he agrees with what is being said and should show his disapproval.

---

1. *Chafetz Chaim* Vol. I, 6:6 and 9:4.

REPENTING FOR HAVING LISTENED TO *LASHON HARA*

If a person transgressed and listened to lashon hara, but did not accept what was said, he must do the following in order to repent.[1]

◆ He must strive to find something favorable in defense of the subject of the conversation and do his best to put the critical things that were said out of his mind.

◆ If he knows that by offering some defense of the subject, the speaker will be even more critical, he should wait until the speaker leaves. Then, he should say something to the subject's credit so that he can help them forget the criticism that was said.

---

1. *Chafetz Chaim* Vol. I, 6:4, see note.

REPENTING FOR HAVING ACCEPTED *LASHON HARA*

If one transgressed and accepted *lashon hara* (i.e., if he believed what was said), he must do the following in order to repent:[1]

◆ He must do his utmost to put what was said out of his mind.

◆ He must accept upon himself not to transgress in the future.

◆ He must confess his sin.

In addition, he should do his utmost to convince the person who spoke the *lashan hara* to overcome his dislike of the subject[2] of the *lashon hara*. (In this way, he rectifies the sin of having placed a stumbling block in front of the blind).

If he repeated what he had heard to others, he must also repent for telling the *lashan hara*, as was explained above.[3]

---

1. *Chafetz Chaim* Vol. I, 6:12.
2. *Chafetz Chaim* Vol. I, 6 and *B'eer Mayim Chaim* ad. loc. 7.
3. *Chafetz Chaim* Vol. I, 6 and *B'eer Mayim Chaim* ad. loc. 34.

REPENTING FOR HAVING SPOKEN *LASHON HARA*

A motivation to facilitate repentance is to study and teach the laws of *lashon hara* and the severity of the sin.

> Question: After having spoken publicly about the enormity of the sin, a man asked me the following. "I know that I have transgressed this sin hundreds of times, and I do not know the names of the people whom I spoke about — thus I cannot ask them for forgiveness. Moreover, because I am a *ben-Torah*, many people learned from me and were not careful in the way they spoke. How can I repent?"
>
> Answer: Our sages said: The righteous earn forgiveness by dealing with the cause of their sins. Therefore, you should try to teach these laws in public, from the works of the authorities who write on the *halachos* of these matters. There, you will find that they are no less important than other Torah prohibitions, and in many ways, are even more severe. All of this should be taught and strengthened. In this manner, you will surely earn the Almighty's forgiveness for what happened in the past, and He will help you avoid stumbling in the future.
>
> *Kuntres K'vod Shomayim*, Chapter 3

THE IMPORTANCE OF STUDYING THE *HALACHOS* OF *LASHON HARA*

Know that the prime manner of avoiding *lashon hara* is not simply accepting upon oneself to avoid speaking. Rather, one must set aside a specific time daily — either a little or a lot — to study the *halachos* and the ethical literature concerning speech. The cure for *lashon hara* is only affected through learning the prohibitions of *lashon hara* and gossip — the general rules as well as specific details as outlined in the Talmud and Midrashic literature. Regarding this type of study, our sages said, "How can one avoid *lashon hara*? By studying Torah." One should also realize that learning the *halachos* of *lashon hara* and gossip only helps those who — while studying — wholeheartedly accept to guard themselves so as not to transgress these prohibitions.

Chovas Hashmirah, Chapter 3

A PRAYER TO BE SAVED FROM THE SIN OF *LASHON HARA*

The following prayer[1] should be recited after *shacharis*. Its recital will serve as a reminder to avoid forbidden speech

רִבּוֹנוֹ שֶׁל עוֹלָם, יְהִי רָצוֹן מִלְּפָנֶיךָ, אֵ-ל רַחוּם וְחַנּוּן, שֶׁתְּזַכֵּנִי הַיּוֹם וּבְכָל יוֹם לִשְׁמֹר פִּי וּלְשׁוֹנִי מִלָּשׁוֹן הָרָע וּרְכִילוּת וּמְקַבְּלָתָם.

וְאֶזָּהֵר מִלְּדַבֵּר אֲפִלּוּ עַל אִישׁ יְחִידִי, וְכָל שֶׁכֵּן מִלְּדַבֵּר עַל כְּלַל יִשְׂרָאֵל, אוֹ עַל חֵלֶק מֵהֶם. וְכָל שֶׁכֵּן מִלְּהִתְרָעֵם עַל מִדּוֹתָיו שֶׁל הַקָּדוֹשׁ בָּרוּךְ הוּא.

וְאֶזָּהֵר מִלְּדַבֵּר דִּבְרֵי שֶׁקֶר, חֲנֻפָּה, לֵצָנוּת, מַחֲלֹקֶת, כַּעַס, גַּאֲוָה, אוֹנָאַת־דְּבָרִים, הַלְבָּנַת־פָּנִים, וְכָל דְּבָרִים אֲסוּרִים.

וְזַכֵּנִי שֶׁלֹּא לְדַבֵּר כִּי־אִם דָּבָר הַצָּרִיךְ לְעִנְיְנֵי גוּפִי אוֹ נַפְשִׁי. וְשֶׁיִּהְיוּ כָּל מַעֲשַׂי וְדִבּוּרַי לְשֵׁם שָׁמָיִם.

---

1. This prayer was formulated by the Chofetz Chaim, and is found at the end of his book, "*Chovas Hashmira*".

TRAINING CHILDREN TO BE CAREFUL OF *LASHON HARA*

It is a *mitzvah* to train one's children and the members of one's household to avoid the sin of *lashon hara*.[1]

◆ One of the reasons why it is so difficult to avoid *lashon hara* is the fact that many of us became accustomed to speaking *lashon hara* as children and even assumed that it was permissible. When we grew up and learned of the prohibition, it became extremely difficult to be careful.

◆ Therefore, it is most important to train one's children. Each and every one of us should speak to the member's of our households[2] about the severity of the prohibition, about the enormity of the punishment to which we are liable and to the great reward that will be given to those who avoid *lashon hara*.

◆ Personal examples are most important. If a person regularly speaks *lashon hara* himself, it will be impossible for him to influence others to avoid it.[3]

---

1. *Chafetz Chaim* Vol. I, 4:10, 8:14 and 9:5.
2. This includes admonishing one's parents—with the utmost respect.
3. One should do all that he can to influence his students as well. If among the students there is a *baal lashon hara* upon whom one has no effect, one should send him away.

REPENTING FOR THE SIN OF *LASHON HARA*

If the subject of the conversation has not as yet suffered any damage, but it is possible that he will in the future	If those listening have accepted what he said and the subject of the conversation became the subject of criticism or suffered either monetary, emotional or physical damage	If those listening have not accepted what he said, and no harm, damage or embarrassment has been caused
↓	↓	↓
It is questionable as to whether he must assuage the feelings of the subject. The speaker should try to convince those who heard what he said, that he was mistaken. The speaker is also culpable for a sin punishable by heaven, and he should therefore**	Even *Yom Kippur* and death do not atone for the sin and he must assuage the subject by asking forgiveness.* Afterwards, he is still culpable for a sin punishable by Heaven and he should therefore	He is culpable for having committed a sin between G-d and himself and to repent, he must:
		1] regret what he has done 2] confess his sin 3] accept upon himself to refrain from committing the sin in the future.

* Even if the subject is unaware of the fact that he was spoken about, the speaker must inform him and ask for his forgiveness.

** If he did not ask the subject to forgive him, and after having repented, damage was caused to the subject as a result of what he had said, he must ask the subject to forgive him.

CHAPTER 12

What is the prohibition of *rechilus* (gossip)?

> The types of speech which are considered *rechilus*
>
> To whom and about whom may one not speak *rechilus*
>
> The prohibition of speech that is considered to have traces of *rechilus*

> R. Yirmiyah bar Abba said: there are four groups of people who do not merit welcoming the *Shechinah* ... [and one of them is] the group that speaks *lashon hara*, as the verse states: *For You are not a G-d who desires evil, wickedness does not dwell in Your presence* (Tehillim 5:5). [The sages explained this to mean] because You are righteous Hashem, evil does not dwell in Your presence.
>
> *Sotah 42a*

WHAT CONSTITUTES PROHIBITED GOSSIP ?

One may not say things which can cause animosity or strife between people. The following are examples of forms of speech that are considered to be *rechilus* (gossip):

- ◆ "Reuven did something that affects you."
- ◆ "Reuven said something about you."
- ◆ "Reuven intends to do something to you."

> Shlomo said: Why does a *metzora* become ritually pure through (use of elements that are taken) from the highest and most simple — from the wood of the cedar and from the hyssop (i.e., a moss that grows on walls)? Man becomes a *metzora* because he acts haughtily like a cedar. By humbling himself like a hyssop, he cures himself with the hyssop.
>
> *P'sikta D'Rav Kehanah* 4

---

1. *Chafetz Chaim* Vol. II, 1:1-2.

WHAT CONSTITUTES PROHIBITED GOSSIP ?

The following are examples of speech that are considered to be *rechilus* (because they can arouse animosity).

◆ One may not repeat to someone, conversations that one heard regarding that person's children, parents or other relatives.[1]

◆ One may not tell a person's wife things that he had heard said about her husband.[2]

◆ If one sees children fighting, one may not inform their parents unless there is a valid purpose in doing so.[3]

◆ One may not say that a person wants to dissolve a partnership, end a *shidduch*, quit a job etc., because this can arouse animosity on the part of the affected party.[4]

---

1. *Chafetz Chaim* Vol. II, 3:3; *B'eer Mayim Chaim* ad. loc. 7.
2. *Chafetz Chaim* Vol. II, 7:3.
3. *Chafetz Chaim* Vol. II, 7:1. If there is a valid purpose, one must be careful to fulfill all of the conditions as outlined in Chapter 16.
4. *Chafetz Chaim* Vol. II, 2:4.

WHAT CONSTITUTES PROHIBITED GOSSIP ?

◆ Speech which causes animosity or strife is prohibited as *rechilus* even though it might not be critical of the subject (and thus not prohibited as *lashon hara*).[1]

◆ Even if the person speaking warns the person listening not to reveal what is said to the subject, the prohibition of *rechilus* applies.[2]

> R. Yehoshua ben Levi said: In what way is a *metzora* different that the Torah requires him to offer two birds (as a sacrifice) in order to become ritually pure? Hashem says: He (the *metzora*) committed a sin by chirping — therefore, the Torah ordains that he offer a sacrifice that chirps.
>
> *Eruvin* 15b

---

1. *Chafetz Chaim* Vol. II, 1:2.
2. *Chafetz Chaim* Vol. II, 3,; *B'eer Mayim Chaim* ad. loc. 7.

ABOUT WHOM MAY ONE NOT SPEAK *RECHILUS* ?

One may not speak *rechilus* about:

◆ a man or a woman.[1]

◆ a relative or stranger.[2]

◆ an adult or a child.[3]

◆ a *talmid chacham* or a simple Jew.[4]

> The verse states: Who is the person who desires life? (... guard your tongue from evil and your lips from speaking deceitfully) (Psalms 34:). Through doing this, every sin will be forgiven, and he will be saved from Sh'eol (purgatory), as the verse states: *One who guards his mouth* (from unnecessary eating and drinking) *and his tongue* (from speaking unnecessarily), *guards his soul from trouble* (Mishlei 21). [And another verse states:] *For death and life are in the power of the tongue* (Mishlei 18). Woe is to him who kills himself because of saying one thing. *And what benefit is there to he who speaks* (Koheles 10:).
>
> *Iggeres Hagra*

---

1. *Chafetz Chaim* Vol. II, 7:1.
2. *Chafetz Chaim* Vol. II, 7:1.
3. *Chafetz Chaim* Vol. II, 7:1.
4. *Chafetz Chaim* Vol. II, 7:2.

THE PROHIBITION OF SPEAKING *RECHILUS* ABOUT *TALMIDEI CHACHAMIM*

Speaking *rechilus* about a *talmid chacham* is considered a very serious transgression.

Rechilus about a spiritual leader can have extremely serious consequences, for aside from the contempt that it brings to the Torah, it can also lead to spiritual degeneration in the community.[1]

> R. Elazar said in the name of R. Yosi ben Zimra: Man has 248 limbs, some of which are upright and some of which are prone. His tongue is encased between two cheeks, his saliva runs below it and the tongue itself is folded and refolded. Yet come and see how many conflagurations it [the tongue] causes. Were it upright, it would surely be so [i.e., it would be able to cause even more damage]. Therefore, Moshe warns Israel and tells them, this is the law of the *metzora*, [i.e., read the word *metzora* as if it said] *motzi shem ra* [i.e., a person who speaks *lashon hara* about others].
>
> *Vayikra Rabba, 16:4*

---

1. *Chafetz Chaim* Vol. II, 7:2.

TO WHOM MAY ONE NOT SPEAK *RECHILUS*?

◆ The prohibition of speaking *rechilus* applies whether one is speaking to a relative or to anyone else.[1]

For example, speaking *rechilus* to one's wife can cause arguments and ongoing strife.

It should be noted that many people are not careful and unwittingly speak *rechilus* when they tell the members of their households what happened at work. Therefore, one should exercise caution even when speaking at home.

> R. Shimon said: If Miriam, the righteous, — who had no intention of speaking *lashon hara* but only intended to speak so as to [bring Moshe and Tzipporah back together so that they might fulfill the *mitzvah*] of being fruitful — received this [punishment of becoming a *metzorah*], evil people who intentionally speak *lashon hara* about their friends so as to destroy their lives, will surely have their tongues cut by Hashem. As the verse states: *May Hashem excise the lips of those who speak smoothly, the tongues of those who boast* (Tehillim 12:4).
>
> *Devarim Rabbah* 6:6

---

1. *Chafetz Chaim* Vol. II, 7:3.

TO WHOM MAY ONE NOT SPEAK *RECHILUS*?

◆ Just as one may not speak *rechilus* to an individual, one may surely not speak *rechilus* to a group of people, for by doing so, one increases the sin.[1]

◆ One may not speak *rechilus* to a Jew and surely not to a gentile, for doing so will cause animosity and strife.[2]

◆ One may not speak *rechilus* to the person who is the subject of the conversation nor to other people, for the conversation will likely reach the ears of those connected to the subject and cause animosity.[3]

---

1. *Chafetz Chaim* Vol.II, 2:1.
2. *Chafetz Chaim* Vol.II, 7:4.
3. *Chafetz Chaim* Vol.II, 3:3 and 7:3.

SPEECH CONSIDERED TO CONSIST OF TRACES OF *RECHILUS*

The following are examples of speech that are considered to be *avak rechilus* (traces of *rechilus*), and as such, Rabbinically proscribed.

◆ One may not tell Reuven, "Shimon spoke *avak lashon hara* about you, when he said, 'I don't want to talk about Reuven'."[1]

◆ One may not say to Reuven, "Why did you refuse to do me a favor? You did the favor for Shimon!"
This type of speech is considered to be *avak rechilus* for it may cause Reuven to hate Shimon for having revealed the fact that Reuven did him a favor.[2]

◆ One may not tell Reuven that Shimon said something about him that can be interpreted either favorably or critically, for doing so may cause Reuven to hate Shimon.[3] Similarly, one may not tell Reuven that Shimon said something about him that was not critical, but is something that people usually prefer not be retold in their presence.[4]

---

1. *Chafetz Chaim* Vol. II, 8:1. See *B'eer Mayim Chaim* ad. loc. 1 who raises the possibility that this type of speech might be considered *rechilus* rather than *avak rechilus*.
2. *Chafetz Chaim* Vol. II, 8:3; *B'eer Mayim Chaim* ad. loc. 4.
3. See *Chafetz Chaim* Vol. II, 2:2 for further examples of this type of speech.
4. *Chafetz Chaim* Vol. II, 8:4.

SPEECH CONSIDERED TO CONSIST OF TRACES OF *RECHILUS*

Speech which may lead the listeners to speak *rechilus* is considered *avak rechilus*.[1]

For example:

One may not praise a person to an extent that might cause those listening to express criticism. One should not, for instance, praise a member of a partnership about the great amount of *tzedakah* that he gives, for the other partner may conclude that the person is wasting their money.

> The Rabbis taught: When R. Eliezer became ill, his students came to visit him. They said to him, "Let our teacher teach us the proper way of life so that we merit the world to come." He replied, "Be careful to [safeguard] the honor of your colleagues and through this you shall merit the world to come."
>
> *Berachoth* 28

---

1. *Chafetz Chaim* Vol. II, 8:2 and *B'eer Mayim Chaim* ad. loc. 2.

CHAPTER 13

When does the prohibition of *rechilus* (gossip) apply?

The prohibition of *rechilus* applies even when the contents of what was said are true, when there was no evil intent, when the matter was already known, etc.

> R. Chama bar Chanina said: How can one rectify the sin of *lashon hara*? If the person who spoke is a *talmid chacham*, he should study Torah for the verse states: *The tree of life heals the tongue* (Mishlei 15:). *The tongue* refers to *lashon hara* as the verse states: *their tongue is like an extended arrow* (Yirmiyah 9:4) and [the word] *tree* refers to the Torah as the verse states: *it is a tree of life for those who grasp it* (Mishlei 3:).
>
> *Arachin* 15b

WHEN ONE IS SPEAKING THE TRUTH, DOESN'T INTEND ANY BAD, OR IS BEING ZEALOUS FOR THE TRUTH

◆ The prohibition of *rechilus* applies even when one is completely telling the truth, and not one word of falsehood is mixed in.[1]

◆ The prohibition of *rechilus* applies even when the speaker does not intend to arouse hatred or discord in the heart of the listener, or to deprecate or cause harm to the person he is speaking about.[2]

◆ Even when the speaker is zealous for the truth and his intentions are worthy, if he has not fulfilled all the conditions required of him to relate the information (see Chapter 17), he has transgressed the prohibition of *rechilus*.[3]

---

1. *Chafetz Chaim* Vol. II, 1:4; 3:1
2. *Chafetz Chaim* Vol. II, 1:3; *B'eer Mayim Chayim* ad. loc. 7
3. *Chafetz Chaim* Vol. I:3, and *B'eer Mayim Chayim* ad. loc. 11.

WHEN THE STORY DOES NOT CONTAIN DEROGATORY CONTENT, OR WHEN THE SUBJECT OF THE CONVERSATION IS PRESENT

The prohibition of *rechilus* applies:

◆ Even in a situation where the subject of the conversation — if confronted — would admit to its accuracy.[1]

◆ Even if the person speaking maintains that the subject of the conversation acted correctly in the situation described.[2]

◆ *Rechilus* is forbidden even when the speaker asserts that he is willing to repeat what he is said in the subject's presence.[1]

◆ It is surely forbidden to speak *rechilus* when speaking in the subject's presence.[3]

---

1. *Chafetz Chaim* Vol. II, 1:2.
2. *Chafetz Chaim* Vol. II, 1:3.
3. *Chafetz Chaim* Vol. II, 3:1 and 6:2.

SITUATIONS WHERE ANIMOSITY ALREADY EXISTS

◆ One may not tell Reuven *rechilus* about Shimon, even if Reuven and Shimon are already at odds with each other because of some other matter (and thus the conversation will not create hatred between them).[1]

◆ Similarly, one may not speak *rechilus* and thereby cause a pre-existing argument to be reignited, for doing so intensifies the strife.[2]

> R. Abba bar Kahana said: the [people who lived during the] generation of King David were all righteous. However, because there were among them people who spoke *lashon hara*, they would go into battle and perish. The generation of Achav, however, were idol worshippers. Since there were no speakers of *lashon hara* among them, they would go into battle and be successful. This is what Ovadyah told Eliyahu HaNavi: *for my master has been told what I did when Ezevel killed the prophets of Hashem ... I provided them with bread and water* (Melachim I, 18:). [since this was a time of extreme drought it was very difficult to find water and even more difficult to keep the matter secret. In spite of this] Eliyahu proclaimed atop Mt. Carmel, *I alone have remained as a prophet to Hashem*, [many people know that there are other prophets] yet they do not report this to the king [which indicates that they were careful not to speak *lashon hara*].
>
> *Yerushalmi Peah 1:1*

---

1. *Chafetz Chaim* Vol. II, 1:4.

WHEN THE INCIDENT IS ALREADY KNOWN OR HAS ALREADY BEEN TOLD

◆ One may not speak *rechilus* even if the person listening is already aware of the incident but could not identify the concerned party without having heard what was now said.[1]

◆ Even if the incident and all of its particulars are already known by the person listening, one may not repeat the *rechilus* if — by doing so — one causes the listener to reconsider the incident and thereby increase his (the listener's) animosity for the subject.[2]

◆ One may not speak *rechilus* even though a previous speaker said the same thing. Though the incident is already known, the fact that it is repeated may very well increase the animosity of those listening.[3]

---

1. *Chafetz Chaim* Vol. II, 1:9.
2. *Chafetz Chaim* Vol. II, 4:1.
3. *Chafetz Chaim* Vol. II, 4:2.

RECHILUS AS A RESULT OF WRITING SOMETHING OR THROUGH INFERENCE EVEN WHEN THE SUBJECT IS NOT IDENTIFIED

The prohibition of *rechilus* applies even if a person wrote about an incident rather than spoke about it.[1]

Moreover, even if he does not specifically speak about an incident, but through hints or inferences he causes strife and hatred, the prohibition of *rechilus* applies.[2]

One may not relate an incident — even if one does not identify the subject. If the subject is later identified, the person who spoke of the incident alone will then be liable for having spoken *rechilus*.[3]

---

1. *Chafetz Chaim* Vol. II, 1:11.
2. *Chafetz Chaim* Vol. II, 1:9.
3. *Chafetz Chaim* Vol. II, 1:9; *B'eer Mayim Chayim* ad. loc. 4.

CHAPTER 14

Avoiding *rechilus*

The importance of avoiding *rechilus* and not speaking *rechilus* even under pressure

> *Life and death are in the hands of the tongue* (Mishlei 18:). What does this verse come to teach me? As Rava said: One who desires life should use his tongue [to study Torah]. And one who desires death should use his tongue [to speak of foolish and obscene matters].
>
> *Arachin* 15a

AVOIDING *RECHILUS*

One should be careful not to ask people "what has so-and-so said about me," because by doing so, he may cause people to speak *rechilus*.[1]

For example, if Shimon told Reuven that Levi spoke critically about him, Reuven may not approach Levi and ask, "Why did you speak critically about me?" Levi will realize that Shimon revealed what he had said, and Reuven will thus be culpable for having caused animosity and strife.[2]

> When the wicked speak *lashon hara*, their speech ascends to the heavenly throne. At that time Gehinnom says to Hashem, "Master of the world, I do not have the ability to punish them in a manner commensurate with what they deserve, and the entire world cannot punish them sufficiently, for the sin of a *baal lashon hara* stretches from the earth to the heavens."
> *Tanna D'Vei Eliyahu Rabbah* 18

---

1. *Chafetz Chaim* Vol. II, 5:5. See also 5:6 and *B'eer Mayim Chaim* ad. loc. 2.
2. *Chafetz Chaim* Vol. II, 3:2.

WHEN PRESSURE IS EXERTED TO SPEAK *RECHILUS*

◆ One may not speak *rechilus* even in situations where intense pressure is exerted upon him to speak.[1]

◆ This is true even if the person pressuring him is his father, teacher or even a king.[1]

◆ Moreover, one may not speak even if those pressuring him are only interested in having him say things which fall into the category of *avak rechilus* (see Chapter 15).[1]

---

1. *Chafetz Chaim* Vol. II, 1:5; *B'eer Mayim Chaim* ad. loc.

SITUATIONS WHEREIN ONE STANDS TO SUFFER GRIEF OR MAY STAND TO LOSE HIS JOB

◆ One may not speak *rechilus* even if as a result of his silence people will curse him and/or cause him much grief.[1]

◆ Moreover, one may not speak *rechilus* even if, as a result of his refusal, he may lose his job and income.[2]

> R. Avahu said: One should always be one of the hunted and not one of the hunters for there are no birds more hunted than the turtle-dove and the Torah made them worthy of being offered [as a sacrifice] on the altar.
> *Bava Kama* 93b

---

1. *Chafetz Chaim* Vol. II, 1:7.
2. *Chafetz Chaim* Vol. II, 1:6; *B'eer Mayim Chaim* ad. loc. 13.

REVEALING MATTERS THAT WERE DECIDED UPON WITHIN A CLOSED FORUM

If a group of people (e.g., a court or government body) decided by majority to find Reuven liable, none of those who were participants may reveal to Reuven that they — or someone else for that matter — had voted to find him innocent.

This is true even if the group did not specifically state that the matter should not be revealed.

Moreover, the prohibition applies even if the person speaking does not say that he voted to find Reuven innocent, but says only that he still feels that Reuven should not be held liable.

[For further clarification, see *Chafetz Chaim* Vol. II, 2:11 and *B'eer Mayim Chaim* ad. loc. As regards revealing secrets, see *Chafetz Chaim* Vol. II, 8:5.]

THE PROPER RESPONSE WHEN ASKED: "WHO DID THIS?" OR "WHAT DID THAT PERSON SAY ABOUT ME ?"

◆ One may not answer this type of question if doing so will cause animosity.

This applies even if the person asked understands that the person asking the question assumes that he was responsible. One should say, "I didn't do it" without stating who was responsible.[1]

◆ If one is asked, "what did someone say about me?", one should respond in a manner that is neither untruthful nor *rechilus*; e.g., by deleting any particulars that could create animosity.[2]

---

1. *Chafetz Chaim* Vol. II, 9:14.
2. *Chafetz Chaim* Vol. II, 1:8; *B'eer Mayim Chaim* ad. loc. 14.

REPENTING FOR HAVING SPOKEN *RECHILUS*

If a person is guilty of having spoken *rechilus*, he is required to ask forgiveness from the person about whom he spoke.

Similarly, he must also repent for the sins against Heaven that are part of the transgression of *rechilus*.[1]

> One should make himself accustomed to honoring all of G-d's creations, for when he recognizes the virtue of the Creator who made man with wisdom, and when he contemplates that they are very deserving of honor, for the Creator Himself made them [he will be careful of speaking critically about them] for by shaming them, he is besmirching the honor of He who created them.
>
> *Tomer D'vorah* 2

---

1. See *Chafetz Chaim* Vol. II, 5:3. See also Chapter 15 regarding doing repentance for having accepted *rechilus*.

CHAPTER 15

The prohibition of accepting *rechilus*

The prohibition of accepting or believing *rechilus* even when what is said seems to be factual.

Our sages taught: [there are] three [people] whom *lashon hara* kills. The person who spoke, the person who accepted [what was said] and the person about whom they spoke [as can be seen from the incident concerning Doeg who was driven from the world because of the *rechilus* he spread about King David, and from the extermination of the residents of Nov, the city of *kohanim*, who were killed because of the *rechilus* spoken about them, and from King Shaul who was later killed because he had accepted *rechilus*]. The person who accepts [*lashon hara* or *rechilus*] is even more culpable than the one who speaks. Our sages added that he who speaks *lashon hara* and he who accepts it deserve to be thrown to the dogs, as the verse states, *Do not take My name in vain* and in proximity [to that verse it says], *and it shall be thrown to the dogs*.

Chafetz Chaim Vol. II, 5:1

THE PROHIBITION OF ACCEPTING *RECHILUS* AND THE OBLIGATION TO JUDGE FAVORABLY

◆ The Torah prohibits believing that the *rechilus* that one heard is true.[1]

◆ Even if subsequent events verify that what was said is indeed true, if there is a possibility of finding grounds to judge the subject favorably (e.g., by assuming that the action spoken about was done inadvertently), the person listening is required to do so.[2]

Further details are outlined in Chapter 7.

> R. Il'ai said, the world only exists [in the merit of] those who remain silent [literally stop] during arguments, as the verse states, *for the world hangs on the stops* (Iyov 26:7).
> *Chullin 89a*

---

1. *Chafetz Chaim* Vol. II, 5:1.
2. See *Chafetz Chaim* Vol. II, 5:6.

WHEN DOES THE PROHIBITION APPLY ?

Generally, in any situation when the speaker is culpable for having transgressed the prohibition of *rechilus*, the listener is also culpable.[1]

At times, the speaker may not be liable (e.g., if he spoke the *rechilus* to accomplish a purpose — see Chapter 16), yet the person listening, who accepts the veracity of what is being said, can still be culpable for having accepted *rechilus*.[2]

> It was taught in the presence of R. Nachman bar Yitzchak, one who embarrasses his friend in public is considered to have murdered him. They said to him, you have spoken well, for we have seen [that the one spoken about] came in with a red face and left with a white face.
>
> *Bava Metzia* 58b

---

1. *Chafetz Chaim* Vol. II, 6; *B'eer Mayim Chaim* ad. loc. 8.
2. *Chafetz Chaim* Vol. II, 6:2. See further details in Chapter 16 regarding the laws of *rechilus* spoken for a purpose.

SITUATIONS WHEN IT SEEMS THAT THE SPEAKER IS TRUTHFUL OR WHEN THERE IS CORROBORATING EVIDENCE

It is prohibited to believe *rechilus* even:

◆ if the person speaking is known to the listener as being as truthful as two witnesses.[1]

◆ if two or more people relate the *rechilus* (which would lend the matter even greater veracity).[2]

The laws applying to accepting *rechilus* in situations when there is corroborating evidence, are brought in the *Chafetz Chaim*.[3]

This situation has a multitude of *halachic* conditions which apply and all of the conditions must be present before one is permitted to accept the *rechilus*.

---

1. *Chafetz Chaim* Vol. II, 6:5-7. It is almost impossible that all of the conditions necessary for one to believe the speech be met. Moreover, nowadays, no-one is considered to have the veracity of two witnesses.
2. *Chafetz Chaim* Vol. II, 6:4.
3. *Chafetz Chaim* Vol. II, 6:6,9-10.

ACCEPTING *RECHILUS* THAT IS WIDELY KNOWN; THE LAW APPLYING TO *RECHILUS* INCIDENTALLY SPOKEN IN A CONVERSATION

(as opposed to *rechilus* which is at the center of the conversation)

One may not believe *rechilus* even if the matter is widely known; e.g.,

◆ even if the story was told in the presence of more than one person.[1]

◆ even if the story was printed and publicized.[1]

◆ even if it is commonly acknowledged that the subect of the *rechilus* did whatever was ascribed to him.[2]

Moreover, one may not believe *rechilus* even if the speaker related what had transpired within the course of a conversation dealing with an entirely different matter (i.e., even though the speaker had no intent of stirring up animosity or strife).[3]

---

1. *Chafetz Chaim* Vol. II, 6:1.
2. *Chafetz Chaim* Vol. II, 6.; *B'eer Mayim Chaim* ad. loc. 5.
3. *Chafetz Chaim* Vol. II, 6:8. It is obviously prohibited to believe *rechilus* that a gentile speaks about a Jew. See *Chafetz Chaim* Vol. II, 6:3 and in the note there.

WHEN THE PEOPLE SPEAKING ARE MEMBERS OF HIS FAMILY

One may not accept *rechilus* even if the person speaking is one's father, mother, wife or other family member.[1]

Many people err and assume that they may believe what is being said since the speaker is a member of the family.

It is right that every person strive that this type of speech should not be prevalent in their homes. He should urge and rebuke those who speak *rechilus* so as to prevent them from continuing.[2]

---

1. *Chafetz Chaim* Vol. II, 6:7 and 7:5.
2. *Chafetz Chaim* Vol. II, 7:5.

IF THE SUBJECT REMAINED SILENT WHEN *RECHILUS* WAS SPOKEN

◆ One may not believe *rechilus* even if it was spoken in the presence of the subject and he remained silent and did not deny what was said.[1]

◆ This is true even if the subject is the kind of person who usually vociferously denies stories that are spread about him. Even though he remained silent in this case, this cannot be taken as proof of the truth of what was said.[1]

◆ Moreover, even in a situation wherein people admonished him and told him that he had done something terribly wrong and he still remained silent, his silence cannot be taken as proof of the veracity of the story.[2]

---

1. *Chafetz Chaim* Vol. II, 6:2.
2. *Chafetz Chaim* Vol. II, 6:8.

ABOUT WHOM MAY ONE NOT ACCEPT *RECHILUS*

One may not accept *rechilus* that is spoken about any Jew.[1]

The laws concerning *rechilus* spoken about a nonbeliever (who is no longer considered a fellow Jew) or about those who are generally considered to be wicked or evil are brought in the Chafetz Chaim.[2]

> R. Shmuel bar Nadav asked R. Chanina... In what way is a *metzora* different than others that the Torah says, *he shall sit alone outside the camp* (Vayikra 13: 46)? [he replied] He [the metzora] separated men and their wives and between men and their fellow man [for his *tzoraas* is a result of speaking *lashon hara*], therefore the Torah said, *he shall sit alone* [i.e., separate from others] *outside the camp*.
>
> *Arachin* 16b

---

1. *Chafetz Chaim* Vol. II, 5:1.
2. *Chafetz Chaim* Vol. II, 6; *B'eer Mayim Chaim* ad. loc. 7.

THE PROHIBITION OF LISTENING TO *RECHILUS*

The Torah prohibits listening to *rechilus* even if one says to himself that he will not accept or believe what is being said as being true.[1]

The prohibition of listening to *rechilus* is in addition to the prohibition of accepting *rechilus* and applies even if the person listening does not accept or believe what is being said.

> R. Chama bar Chanina said, what is the meaning of the verse that states, *for death and life are in the power* [literally *in the hands*] *of the tongue* (Mishlei 18:21)? Does the tongue have a hand? Rather, the verse teaches us just as a hand can kill, so too can the tongue kill. However, I would assume that just as a hand can only kill things that are in its proximity, so too can the tongue kill only that which is in its proximity. The verse therefore states, *for their tongues are like killing arrows* (Yirmiyahu 9:7). However, I would assume that just as an arrow can kill at a distance of 40 or 50 cubits, so too can the tongue kill only that which is at a distance of 40 or 50 cubits. The verse therefore states, *for their mouths drink in the heaven, and their tongues walk on earth* (Tehilim 73:9).
>
> Arachin 15b

---

1. *Chafetz Chaim* Vol. II, 5:2. The laws of *rechilus* spoken to achieve a purpose are detailed in Chapter 17.

REPENTING FOR HAVING ACCEPTED *RECHILUS*

If a person transgressed and accepted *rechilus*, he must do the following:[1]

◆ Drive what was said out of his mind and not believe the story to be true (or at least say to himself that the speaker exaggerated, omitted details or blew things out of their proper proportion).

◆ Make a resolution not to accept *rechilus* in the future.

◆ Confess his transgression.

If he repeated the *rechilus* to others, he is required to repent for having spoken *rechilus*[2] as outlined in Chapter 12.

---

1. *Chafetz Chaim* Vol. II, 5:7.
2. *Chafetz Chaim* Vol. II, 4:3.

CHAPTER 16

The laws regarding *rechilus* spoken for a purpose

The *halachos* applicable to *rechilus* when there is a purpose in listening.

> Hashem said, in this world, because you did not speak words of Torah, you spoke about your fellow man. In the world to come, however, you shall learn Torah taught by Me, and I will increase harmony amongst you.
>
> *Yalkut Shimoni* to *B'haaloscha* 5742

WHEN THERE IS A CONSTRUCTIVE PURPOSE INVOLVED

◆ If there is a constructive purpose involved in listening to *rechilus*, one may listen; e.g. so as to avoid or be careful of becoming involved with someone.[1]

◆ If a person has reason to fear (based on real rather than imaginary reasons) that someone wishes to do him harm, he may investigate that person so as to exercise caution.[2]

The person investigating need not fear that people will tell him *lashon hara* or *rechilus*, since his purpose in investigating is constructive. However, when making inquiries, he must make it clear that he has a constructive purpose. Moreover, he may not believe what is said but may only accept what is said as a basis for exercising caution.

---

1. *Chafetz Chaim* Vol. II, 5:2. See also 5:6 and *B'eer Mayim Chaim* ad. loc. 2.
2. See *Chafetz Chaim* Vol. II, 5:3 and *B'eer Mayim Chaim* ad. loc. 4.

WHEN THERE IS A CONSTRUCTIVE PURPOSE INVOLVED

If a person is about to develop a relationship with another person (e.g., a partnership or a *shidduch*), he may investigate the other person so as to avoid damages, strife, a *chilul Hashem* et. al.[1]

Again, when investigating he must make it clear to those whom he approaches that he is investigating so as to accomplish a constructive purpose. In this manner, those who answer his inquiries will not be liable for having spoken *rechilus* and/or *lashon hara*.

When conducting this type of an investigation, one should not make inquiries of people who bear animosity towards the subject of the investigation.

> There are three [types of people] whom Hashem loves: he who does not become angry ... and he who does not bear a grudge.
> *Pesachim* 113b

---

1. See *Chafetz Chaim* Vol. II, 5:3 and *B'eer Mayim Chaim* ad. loc.

ONE MAY NOT BELIEVE WHAT IS SAID EVEN IF ONE IS LISTENING SO AS TO ACCOMPLISH A CONSTRUCTIVE PURPOSE

Even if one is making inquiries so as to accomplish a constructive purpose, one may still not believe what is said.

The information that is related should be used only as a basis for being careful but may not be accepted as fact since every person is considered to be good unless proven otherwise.[1]

Similarly, one may not cause harm or embarrassment to the subject nor may one bear animosity towards him.[2] One may not use the information as a reason to avoid paying one debts to a person even if the information one received indicates that the subject caused him financial loss.[3] Additionally, despite the information that was received, one is still dutybound to extend to the subject, all of the help that the Torah requires. [4]

---

1. *Chafetz Chaim* Vol. II, 5:1-4 and 6:1.
2. *Chafetz Chaim* Vol. II, 5:4.
3. *Chafetz Chaim* Vol. II 5:4; *B'eer Mayim Chaim* ad. loc. 7.
4. *Chafetz Chaim* Vol. II, 5:4.

WARNING SOMEONE TO AVOID A PERSON

Reuven is informed that Shimon is about to establish a relationship with Levi (e.g., a partnership, rental agreement[1] or *shidduch*), and Reuven has reason to believe that the relationship will cause damage to Shimon. If the relationship has not yet been formed[2] (i.e., by means of a form of contractual agreement binding according to the Torah), Reuven is required to inform Shimon. However, the following preconditions apply.[3]

A. Reuven must be certain that the proposed relationship is indeed damaging.

B. Reuven may not exaggerate when relating the information to Shimon.

C. Reuven must be certain that his motive in telling Shimon is to accomplish a constructive purpose rather than based on his animosity for Levi. (If Shimon is the type of person who will relate what Reuven tells him to others, Reuven may not relate the information.)[4]

---

1. *Chafetz Chaim* Vol. II, 9:1; *B'eer Mayim Chaim* ad. loc. 3.
2. *Chafetz Chaim* Vol. II, 9:5.
3. *Chafetz Chaim* Vol. II, 9:2.
4. See *B'eer Mayim Chaim* ad. loc. 5.

WARNING SOMEONE TO AVOID A PERSON (cont.)

D. If there is another means of conveying the information to Shimon, Reuven should employ it rather than telling Shimon.

E. Relating the story should only serve to dissolve the proposed relationship, but not cause additional damages to Levi.

F. If Reuven did not personally witness the incident that he is relating, it is questionable as to whether he may inform Shimon. In any event, he must make it clear that he did not witness the incident that he is relating.[1]

---

1. See *B'eer Mayim Chaim* ad. loc. 9.

WARNING SOMEONE AFTER THE RELATIONSHIP WAS FORMED

If Shimon already entered into the relationship with Levi (through one of the contractual forms of agreement outlined by the Torah), Reuven may only inform Shimon[1] of what he knows if he is certain that Shimon will not act in a manner prohibited by the Torah (e.g., dissolving the partnership) but will only exercise caution. The conditions outlined previously, apply in this case as well.

If Reuven knows that as a result of telling Shimon, Levi will suffer damages greater than those due him for whatever he has done, Reuven may not inform Shimon.

The *halacha* is more complex if two people witnessed the incident concerning Levi.[2]

---

1. *Chafetz Chaim* Vol. II, 9:1,5; *B'eer Mayim Chaim* ad. loc. 17.
2. See *Chafetz Chaim* Vol. II, 9.